Steve & Maryann

You Both are a inspiration & blessing to me and my whole family. Praying for you all & hope to see you all Soon! Hope this is a book of Joy & Future blessings.

Love you
Gigi, Nikki, & Zach

The **Blessed** Life

The Blessed Life
Copyright © 2002, 2015 Gateway Create Publishing
All rights reserved.

Gateway Church edition published in 2002.
Regal Books edition published in September 2004.
Gateway Church special edition published in January 2015.

Written by Robert Morris
Art Director Shane Dennehey
Design Emanuel Puscas
Production Design Katrina Sirmon
Photographer Cory Hale
Edited by Mia Kaely (2002), Daniel Hopkins (2015)

Requests for information should be addressed to:
Gateway Create Publishing, 810 Mustang Dr, Ste 300, Grapevine, TX 76051

Unless otherwise indicated, all Scripture citations are taken from the New King James Version. Copyright © 1979, 1980, 1982 by Thomas Nelson, Inc. Used by permission. All rights reserved.

Scripture citations marked KJV are taken from the Authorized King James Version.

Scripture citations marked NIV are taken from the Holy Bible New International Version® NIV®. Copyright © 1973, 1978, 1984, 2011 by Biblica, Inc.™ Used by permission of Zondervan. All rights reserved.

Scripture citations marked NLT are taken from the Holy Bible, New Living Translation, Copyright © 1996, 2004. Used by permission of Tyndale House Publishers, Inc., Wheaton, Illinois 60189. All rights reserved.

Appendix was adapted from The Blessed Life: A Companion Study Guide to the Book and Teaching Series, also by Robert Morris (Southlake, Texas: Gateway Church, 2003).

Library of Congress Cataloging-in-Publication Data
Morris, Robert (Robert Preston), 1961–
The blessed life / Robert Morris.
p. cm.
Includes bibliographical references.
ISBN 0-8307-3635-2 (hardcover), ISBN 0-8307-3673-5 (trade paper)
1. Christian giving. I. Title.
BV772.M634 2004
248'.6—dc22
2004012726

Any Internet addresses (websites, blogs, etc.) and telephone numbers in this book are offered as a resource. They are not intended in any way to be or imply an endorsement by Gateway Create Publishing, nor does Gateway Create Publishing vouch for the content of these sites or accuracy of phone numbers for the life of this book.

Some names and details of actual events have been changed to protect the identities of the persons involved.

Printed in the United States of America.

the
BLESSED
Life

UNLOCKING THE REWARDS
OF GENEROUS LIVING

ROBERT MORRIS
SPECIAL EDITION FEATURING A 21-DAY DEVOTIONAL

CONTENTS

FOREWORD

It was like a breath of fresh air to Betty and me when we heard Robert Morris, senior pastor of Gateway Church in the Dallas/Fort Worth area, teach so effectively, biblically, and accurately on the subject of giving. I believe Robert has hit the target dead center and captured the heart of God.

For the last 10 years, I have had the opportunity to witness the undeniable, profound impact *The Blessed Life* message has had on the 36,000 people attending Gateway Church. I have hosted many pastors and laypersons on *LIFE Today* who have also testified of the transforming power Robert's teaching has had in their own lives. Over the years I had become so disappointed by the manipulative tactics of some ministries that I had been very reluctant to share in depth my own deep convictions concerning giving and receiving. *The Blessed Life* has provided the opportunity to share this great truth.

The law of the harvest is irrefutable and we will unquestionably reap what we sow. However, I don't believe in leading people to focus on their own gain without understanding the sheer joy of living to give and loving to share. Jesus clearly said, "It is more blessed to give than to receive" (Acts 20:35), so it puzzles me when I hear ministers and evangelists place the major focus on how we can *get, get, get*. This kind of teaching leads people to believe that by giving or sowing seed, they are going to reap a money tree in their backyard. It's like playing spiritual bingo or the lottery.

Betty and I have spent our entire 51 years of marriage enjoying the thrill of giving, and I can say with no exaggeration that we have *never* given one time to any person, ministry, or a specific need thinking we will surely get a return. Even if there is no immediate visible return, the delightful joy of giving and seeing its positive effect should continually inspire us to give.

Is there any question that those who give for the right reason and with the right heart do often gain or receive a return? No question about it. The problem is the focus of the heart. We put our treasure where our heart is (Matthew 6:20-21).

God is interested in creating the heart of a farmer. A farmer prepares the soil, plows, plants, carefully oversees, and seeks to protect what he has planted but trusts God for the increase in due season. If he doesn't see it come at an expected time, he knows in due season it will. If he's hailed out, rained out, stormed out, or droughted out, he still farms because he has the heart of a farmer. Many people talk about the promise of "a hundredfold" return (Matthew 13:8, 23). The truth is, not every farmer receives that kind of return.

We often go through trials, tests, and tribulations that are almost unbearable while we continue to be faithful to the Lord. However, we must recognize that everything we have belongs to God, and we are merely the stewards. It's easy to place what belongs to somebody else in the proper areas. If, however, we have the attitude of the rich fool and try to guard it, hoard it, protect it, keep it, and think only of ourselves, we haven't for one moment identified with the heart of God.

If you want to be set free in the area of giving and learn what it really means to discover the truth of "Give, and it will be given to you: good measure, pressed down, shaken together, and running over" (Luke 6:38), then read what Pastor Robert shares throughout these pages. Remember, the focus will be on God and others and very little on self.

Does it mean that we don't care if we don't have a return? Does it mean that we don't ever hope to receive? As surely as a farmer hopes for the harvest and is confident it will come in due season, it does matter. But the focus can't be there. We've got to lose sight of self and understand the value of giving and sharing in order to live like a river.

As one very successful businessman said to a small group at lunch one day, "I feel I'm like a river. No matter how much I give, I never have less; no matter how much I receive, I never have any more." What he receives, he releases into the purposes of God. That does not mean that this individual could not have had a nicer car, a more expensive suit, or a bigger house. It simply means he is not controlled by what God has entrusted to him and what he has received. He is continually releasing what God gives him, and he has become a conduit and expression of God's love.

May God bless you as you read this book.

James Robison
Founder and President
LIFE Outreach International
Fort Worth, Texas

INTRODUCTION

I can say with absolute confidence that Satan does not want you to read this book. Without a doubt, the enemy of your soul would do anything to keep you from discovering God's principles governing financial stewardship, giving, and blessing. Why? Because once you do, it will transform your life for the better. It will bring you guaranteed financial results. But it will also do more than that: It will impact the kingdom of God.

You see, if every believer understood and applied the simple principles I am about to present, it would literally bring revival to the world. Every needed church facility could be built. Every missionary with a divine call and a willing heart could be sent and abundantly supplied. The gospel could saturate every culture on the planet.

Yes, as God's people prospered, money would come into the kingdom; but much more important, our hearts would be changed!

That's why I am so pleased (and the devil isn't!) that you have picked up this book. Through these extraordinary truths, God will do an amazing work in your heart. He will change you forever. And, I promise, you will like it.

No one is a natural-born giver. We are all born takers. We enter this world with a fallen sin nature, and at the heart of that nature is a tendency toward selfishness.

In contrast, God is a giver. The most widely known verse in the Bible tells us:

For God so loved the world that He gave His only begotten Son (John 3:16).

God is generous beyond our ability to imagine. But it was selfishness and pride that caused Satan to be cast out of heaven.

Many people in our culture have that exactly backward. They see God as stingy and the devil as the one who likes to pass out favors. So, if you are ever prone to getting confused about this issue, remember it this way: God and *generous* both begin with the letter G. Satan and *selfish* both begin with S. That should help you keep it straight!

To be serious for a moment, I am very excited for you. You are about to begin a journey of discovery. I can tell you from personal experience, there is no greater adventure on earth than simply living the life of generosity and abundance that is available to all of God's people—but that so few ever dare to live. It is a journey of reward. It is *the blessed life.*

Read on, and let the adventure begin!

THE UNEXPECTED ADVENTURE

T he odometer on our "highly experienced" station wagon showed upwards of 130,000 miles as I rolled up to the pump at a little gas station in Oklahoma. It was 1984, and I was a young evangelist. In those days, my wife, Debbie, and I would gladly drive to just about any place that would offer me an opportunity to preach.

We were on a journey that day in two senses of the word. Yes, we were on our way to minister the gospel. But this little filling station was also a stop on a voyage of discovery—one we had embarked upon about a month earlier. It was a journey into the power and joy of Spirit-led giving.

As I walked into the station to pay for my gasoline, the lady behind the counter said, "It's taken care of."

"Excuse me?" I asked, a little confused.

"It's taken care of," she repeated. "You don't owe anything for the gas."

Now I was genuinely confused. "Why is that?"

Very matter-of-factly, she said, "When you pulled up, God told me that you were an evangelist and that I was to pay for your gas. So it's taken care of."

Grateful and still a little startled, I thanked her warmly and went on my way.

That stop was a small but significant milestone on this journey I mentioned. The idea that the Spirit of God would speak to someone and instruct them to give wasn't a new concept for me. In fact, this incident was a perfect example of the very thing God had begun to make a centerpiece of my ministry and my walk as a Christian.

THE NEXT LEVEL

As a traveling evangelist, all of my income came from the love offerings I received from the churches in which I preached. In those years, my income from offerings might be $800 one week and $200 the next. Debbie and I just never knew. But early in our marriage, we had learned to trust God where our finances were concerned.

We were diligent tithers. God had spoken clearly to us about the principle of the tithe several years earlier. And ever since we began honoring the Lord by giving the first tenth of everything that came in, our needs have always been met—sometimes miraculously. What we didn't know was that God was about to take us to the next level.

As I mentioned, about a month before the surprise blessing at the gas station, God did something remarkable to get my attention where the matter of giving was concerned.

I was scheduled to preach at a church for only one night, and as it turned out, it was the only meeting I was scheduled to preach at all month. From a financial standpoint, that meant having only one opportunity to receive an offering instead of the usual four, five, or six. Although Debbie and I had grown in our ability to trust and rest in God, this represented a major budgeting challenge in the making.

At the close of the service, the church received a love offering on my behalf. Shortly thereafter, the pastor approached me with an envelope.

He said, "Robert, I'm pleased and amazed to tell you that this is the largest love offering this little church has ever given. God used you to bless us tonight, and I'm so happy to be able to give this to you."

When I opened the envelope, I found a check for roughly the same amount as our entire monthly budget. In one meeting, God had miraculously provided what it normally took several meetings to produce. It was quite a lesson for us. But the lesson wasn't over yet.

As I stood there holding that check, basking in the warm glow of gratitude and wonder, something happened to me that forever changed the course and quality of my life.

Earlier in that evening's service, a missionary had given a brief testimony and update for the congregation. Now, as I looked across the nearly empty sanctuary, I caught sight of him. As I did, the unmistakable voice of the Lord spoke in my heart, *I want you to give him your offering—all of it.*

In an instant, I went from euphoria to something approximating panic. *Lord, that can't be Your voice! I mean ... after all ... I ... You ... You just did a miracle here to meet our needs!*

Once again, the instruction came through, gently but clearly. *I want you to give him your offering.*

Like a kid who doesn't want to hear what his brother is saying, I wanted to stick my fingers in my ears and sing loudly, "La, La, La, La, La ... ! What? I can't hear you!"

Give him the whole offering. Trust Me.

I couldn't shake it off. I tried to rationalize. I tried bargaining. I tried begging. The impression only grew stronger.

Ultimately, I waved the white flag and said, "Okay, Father, I trust You." I endorsed the back of the check, folded it in half, and took a quick glance around the room to make sure no one was watching.

Walking up to the missionary, I said something like, "I really appreciated your testimony tonight. Please, don't tell anyone about this, but I would like you to have this offering. The check is made out to me, but I have signed it over to you." I handed him the check and walked away.

An hour later, I found myself seated with about 20 members of the church at a pizza place. Across from me sat a well-dressed man I barely knew. (We had met briefly on one other occasion.)

After a while, he leaned across the table toward me, looked me straight in the eye, and asked me a shockingly personal question, "How much was your offering tonight?"

Naturally, his question flustered me. I had never had anyone ask me that before, especially a near stranger! His boldness so caught me off guard that I didn't know what else to do but answer him. So, I told him the amount of the offering. I remember hoping that was the end of it. It wasn't.

In the same authoritative manner, he asked me another question, "Where is the check?" *What nerve!* I remember thinking. *What is he up to?*

Of course, I no longer had the check, but I wasn't about to tell him that. So, I am not proud to tell you, this preacher lied through his teeth.

"Uh ... my wife has it," I said nervously. She was sitting at the other end of the long table—a nice, safe distance away. *Now can we change the subject?!*

"Go get it. I want to see it." The man was relentless! Not knowing what else to do, I made a pretense of getting up to go ask her for the check. Bending down close to her ear, I asked, "How's your pizza?" "Good," she replied, giving me a perplexed look. "Great. Glad to hear it. Just checking," I muttered and headed back down the table to my seat.

My ears heard another lie floating past my lips. "She left it out in the car," I said, trying to make the car sound as if it was very, very far away. (At this point, not only was I trying to hide the fact that I had given my whole love offering away, but I was also covering the fact that this evangelist, who had just spent the evening proclaiming that Jesus is the way, the truth, and the life, had just lied!)

As tiny beads of perspiration began to pop out on my face, the gentleman leaned across the table and got uncomfortably close. "The check's not in the car, Robert," he stated in a low voice.

"How do you know that?" I responded, trying to sound a little offended.

"Because God told me—and He told me something else."

At that point, the man spoke words that have rolled like thunder through my life ever since.

"God is about to teach you about giving so that you can teach the body of Christ." With that, he slid a folded piece of paper across the table. It was a check. The amount—to the penny—was 10 times the amount of the one I had given away only an hour or so earlier.

Ten times—to the penny.

That was the night this journey started.

WONDERS OF PROVISION

"God wants to teach you about giving so that you can teach the body of Christ." Those words stayed at the forefront of our minds in the amazing months that followed. Debbie and I were wide open to anything God wanted to teach us. And, as a result, we saw God work wonders of provision over and over.

Sometimes He would prompt us to trust Him and give. Other times, He would use someone else to bless us unexpectedly.

For example, not long after that life-changing night, Debbie and I were at an in-home Bible study where we spoke with a couple who was about to leave on a missionary trip. They had asked us to pray for them before they left. They particularly requested prayer for their finances. "We don't quite have all the money this trip will require," they told us. They did not mention the amount needed but, as we prayed, I had a strong impression that the amount was $800.

At that point in our lives, $800 sounded like a very large sum of money. But we had it, because of the amazing tenfold blessing we had received at the pizza place.

That night, we were able to walk out to our car after the meeting and write a check. We caught them before they drove away and handed it to them. Of course, it was the precise amount they needed to be able to take that mission trip.

Frankly, it was the most exciting thing Debbie and I had ever done. We were quickly beginning to discover how thrilling it is to be able to give when God tells us to do so.

Within the next few weeks, we had the encounter at the gas station I related at the beginning of this chapter.

Shortly after that, we went out to eat with a man who had just purchased a new van. We all rode in it to the restaurant and were talking about how nice the van was and how excited for him we were. When we returned to his home, he said, "Help me get my stuff out of my van," so I began to gather up his cassette tapes and other items he pointed out. After several trips, I asked, "Do you even want that umbrella out of there? And, by the way, why are you moving all this stuff inside?"

His response was, "Because I'm giving you the van. But I need my umbrella!" "Excuse me?" I asked. He repeated, "I'm giving you this van. God told us to."

Naturally, we were awestruck, grateful, and thrilled. The brand-new van had a value of more than $25,000!

Of course, that blessing raised another question. Now that we have this van, what do we do with the station wagon? It wasn't much to look at, but it was good, reliable transportation.

After some prayer, we felt the Lord instructing us to give the station wagon to a family that we knew didn't have a vehicle.

Almost immediately, someone we didn't even know gave us another vehicle! "God told us to" was the familiar explanation.

After more prayer, we gave that vehicle away as well. Soon, another one arrived to replace it. And then another one. And another one. Each time a vehicle landed in our driveway, we would give it away. And each time, another one would show up to take its place.

In the middle of this amazing sequence, God did something that, at first, puzzled us. In the case of one of the cars we were given, our prayer for direction brought this instruction from the Lord: *Don't give this vehicle away. Sell it.*

At first, we weren't sure we had heard God accurately. Seeking confirmation, we said, "Lord, are You sure You want us to sell this vehicle? We certainly have enjoyed giving them away."

The clear reply came back, *No, I want you to sell the vehicle. I want you to sell it for $12,000.*

At church that weekend, a man walked up to me and said, "Hey Robert, would you like to sell that van?" Somewhat startled, I said, "Yes, as a matter of fact, I believe I'm supposed to sell it." The man then said, "I think the Lord wants me to give you $12,000 for it. Is that acceptable?" Of course, I sold him the vehicle.

The very next week we were scheduled to go on a mission trip to Costa Rica, so we put the $12,000 in the bank, awaiting instructions from the Lord on what to do with it.

A few days later, we found ourselves in Costa Rica riding in a dilapidated old van owned by the missionary we were there to assist. I was genuinely concerned about whether we were going to make it to our destination.

At one point, I asked the missionary, "Why don't you buy a new van? I think this one is about to die and go to be with the Lord!"

"As a matter of fact, I *am* about to get a new van!" the missionary said very excitedly. "Last week, I was driving by a car lot, and the Lord told me to stop. Then He pointed out a van to me and said, 'I want to give you that van, so I want you to pray over it'; so I did! I don't know how the Lord is going to give me that van," he continued, "but I know He will!"

Sensing the hand of God, I asked him, "How much do they want for it?" I'm sure you have already guessed the answer: $12,000. With great joy, my wife and I were able to write the check for $12,000 as soon as we got home.

OUTGIVE GOD?

Throughout this remarkable season of giving, we experienced tremendous blessing. Our income had skyrocketed. It seemed the more we gave, the more God gave to us. It was as if we were truly living out the old saying: You can't outgive God.

Over the course of those 18 months, it was our privilege to give away nine vehicles. What's more, we were able to increase our giving to 70 percent of our gross income. We found ourselves living more comfortably on 30 percent than we previously had on 90 percent.

You can't outgive God.

We simply encountered God's blessings everywhere we turned. And around each corner, we learned new lessons in the power of Spirit-led giving. Just when we thought we were as radical about giving as we could possibly be, God would stretch us a little bit more.

For example, toward the end of that 18-month period, the Lord spoke to us about giving both of our vehicles away. He said, "I want you to give them both away. I'll show you the couple to whom you are to give them; and another thing, I also want you to give your house away; and I also want you to take every bit of money that you have in the bank and give it away too."

Needless to say, we wrestled with this one. When we prayed, we said, "Lord, You're asking us to give everything away that we own. Are You sure this is what You're saying?" And the Lord kept saying, "I'm sure, I'm sure."

So we did. As the Lord showed us the recipients, we gave the vehicles away. We gave away all the money in our bank accounts. And we looked and listened diligently for instructions about giving away the house. In our hearts, we had already given the house away. We had fully released it. We just needed to know to what family we were to hand the title and the keys.

There we were—without transportation and without a dollar with which to buy any. As I sat in my house (which I no longer considered to be mine), I have to admit, I was having some carnal thoughts.

I remember thinking to myself, *Aha! I've got Him. This time I've outgiven the Lord!*

I recall having a very frank and honest discussion with God, saying, "Lord, You know, I think I've outgiven You this time. Yes, every time we gave a car away, You gave us another car. Well, this time, I've given both my vehicles and all my money away! This time, I think I've got You, Lord. I've outgiven You."

Even as I said that, I sensed in my heart the Lord saying, *Oh, really!* At that moment, the telephone rang. On the other end of the line was a man who said, "Robert, God has spoken to me about helping you with your transportation." (You need to know that, besides the recipients, no one on earth knew of what Debbie and I had given. This man did not know we had given our vehicles away.)

My immediate thought was, *Well, that's a blessing. This man is going to give us a car.* My assumption was that the pattern we had seen repeat itself so many times was about to play out once more. I must also admit that I thought, *Well, Lord, even if he gives us a car, the fact remains that we gave away two cars, all of our money and, in effect, our house. So I think I've still got You.*

So I asked the man on the phone, "What did the Lord tell you to do?" He answered, "The Lord told me to buy you an airplane." I was speechless.

He continued, "As a matter of fact, I bought the plane today; *and* I've parked it at the airport; *and* I'm going to pay for the hangar; *and* I'm going to pay for the fuel; *and* I'm going to pay for the insurance and maintenance on the airplane; *and* I've hired a pilot. I'm going to pay his salary, so anytime you want to go somewhere, just call him and he'll fly you there. I'll take care of all the expenses!"

As I stood there stammering and stunned, I heard the still, small voice of the Lord whisper in my spirit, "Gotcha."

My friend, you can't outgive God.

God offers the only true guaranteed financial results available on earth. There are principles, however, that we have to follow in order to experience God's highest rewards.

They are the keys to living the blessed life.

BLESSED OR CURSED?

Before we continue, I should probably define terms. What do I mean by "the blessed life?" What does a life filled with blessing look like?

Being "blessed" means having supernatural power working for you. By contrast, being "cursed" means having supernatural power working against you.

The days of the blessed person are filled with divine "coincidences" and heavenly meaning. A blessed man may or may not be wealthy by the world's standards, but he enjoys a quality of life that most billionaires would envy.

> *Being "blessed" means having supernatural power working for you.*

At four separate points in the book of Deuteronomy, God tells those who will obey Him that He will bless everything to which they put their hands (see 14:29; 15:10; 23:20; 28:8, 12). That's what the blessed life is like. Everything you touch does well.

Blessing permeates every aspect of a person's life—health, relationships, work, family, emotions, and thoughts.

Sound good? Then read on. You're about to discover how to live a life of blessing.

GOD MUST
BE FIRST

We've heard the old saying many times: First things first.

There is a heap of biblical truth in that little cliché. So what are the "first things" where living the blessed life is concerned? Well, consider this: There are more than 500 verses in the Bible concerning prayer and nearly 500 verses concerning faith, but more than 2,000 verses on the subject of money and possessions.

Jesus talked about money in 16 of His 38 parables. Clearly, from the Bible's standpoint, we need to understand money and how to handle it. Why? Because money is actually a test from God.

How you handle money reveals volumes about your priorities, loyalties, and affections. In fact, it directly dictates many of the blessings you will (or won't) experience in life.

The very first principle you must grasp, if you are to understand giving, is the principle of firstfruits. It can also be called the principle of the firstborn or the tithe.

Frankly, far too many Christians are confused about tithing and the principle of firstfruits. (Please don't tune me out, turn me off, or skip these pages, thinking, *I've heard all that tithing stuff before.* There is life-giving, liberating truth in what I am about to present to you. Don't miss it!)

SACRIFICED OR REDEEMED

We find an important financial precedent established in the thirteenth chapter of Exodus. In this passage, God says:

> Consecrate to Me all the firstborn, whatever opens the womb among the children of Israel, both of man and beast; it is Mine (Exodus 13:2).

Here, God plainly declares that the firstborn "is Mine." It belongs to Him. In fact, you'll find God declaring 16 times in Scripture that the firstborn is His! For example, Exodus 13:12-13 says:

> That you shall set apart to the Lord all that open the womb, that is, every firstborn that comes from an animal which you have; the males shall be the Lord's. But every firstborn of a donkey you shall redeem with a lamb; and if you will not redeem it, then you shall break its neck. And all the firstborn of man among your sons you shall redeem.

It is vital that you understand something about the principle of the firstborn. According to Old Testament law, the firstborn was to be either sacrificed or redeemed. There was no third option. Every time one of your livestock animals delivered its firstborn, you were to sacrifice it, or if it was designated unclean, you had to redeem it with a clean, spotless lamb. To summarize, the clean firstborn had to be sacrificed and the unclean firstborn had to be redeemed.

With that in mind, think about the account in the New Testament in which John the Baptist meets Jesus on the banks of the Jordan River.

John was baptizing one day and looked up to see Jesus walking toward him. At that point, John cried out, "Behold! The Lamb of God who takes away the sin of the world!" (John 1:29).

Jesus was God's tithe.

With that inspired declaration, John perfectly defined the role Jesus had come to fulfill. Jesus was God's firstborn. Jesus was clean—perfect and unblemished in every way. On the other hand, every one of us was born unclean. We were all born sinners with a fully active sin nature.

Now think back to the principle of the firstborn in Exodus. Remember, the law stated that if the firstborn animal was clean, it was to be sacrificed. But if the firstborn was unclean, it was to be redeemed with a clean animal.

Do you see the symbolic parallel? Jesus Christ was God's firstborn Son, and He was born clean. He was born a pure, spotless lamb. But every one of us was born unclean; therefore, Jesus was sacrificed to redeem us.

When He redeemed us by His sacrifice, He bought us back for God. He was literally a firstfruits offering. In a very real sense, Jesus was God's *tithe*.

God gave His tithe (Jesus) in faith before we ever believed. Notice that God gave Him to us *before* we believed. Romans 5:8 says:

> God demonstrates His own love toward us, in that while we were still sinners, Christ died for us.

We have to give our firstfruits offering—our tithes—in much the same way. *Before* we see the blessing of God, we give it in faith.

God gave Jesus in faith "that He might be the firstborn among many brethren" (Romans 8:29). In this sense, Jesus is God's tithe. God gave Jesus first, in faith, even when we were sinners—even as we were mocking Him and spitting in His face while He was dying.

God didn't wait to see if we would first change or repent or make ourselves worthy. God knew the principle of first things first.

Have you ever wondered how God could justify taking the lives of Egypt's firstborn in the final plague described in Exodus? It is because the firstborn belongs to God. God had a legal right to take every firstborn because every one of them in Egypt and in Israel belonged to Him!

But the firstborn in Israel didn't die that night, did they? Why not? Because a lamb was sacrificed to redeem them. A spotless, perfect Lamb took their place!

You'll recall that God instructed Moses to apply the blood of the sacrificed lamb to the doorposts of each home. They were to apply the blood to the mantle (the top of the doorframe) and on the posts (the sides of the doorframe) (see Exodus 12:7).

Imagine yourself standing outside one of those doors, dipping a hyssop branch in that lamb's blood. See yourself applying the blood, first on the left side of the doorframe, then going across and applying it on the right side and then reaching up and applying the blood in the middle of the mantle, on the top, so the blood would drip down.

Did you notice that, in following those steps, you created the form of a cross in blood? The Israelites were saved by the blood of the lamb in the form of a cross! And that's precisely how we're saved. God redeemed us in the same way—by giving His firstborn Son as a sacrifice.

The principle of the firstfruits is very, very powerful. I have heard it said that any first thing given is never lost, and any first thing not given is always lost. In other words, what we give to God, we don't lose because God redeems it for us. But what we withhold from God, we will lose. Jesus echoed this principle when He said:

> For whoever wants to save his life will lose it, but whoever loses his life for me will find it (Matthew 16:25, NIV).

The first belongs to God. We find this principle all through God's Word. We can give God the first of our time. We can give Him the first of our finances. That's what tithing really is—giving our first to God. It's saying, "God, I'm going to give to You first and trust You to redeem the rest."

Put another way, when a firstborn lamb is born in a flock, it is not possible to know how many more lambs that ewe might produce. Nevertheless, God didn't say, "Let your ewe produce nine lambs first, and then give Me the next one." No, God says, "Give Me the first one."

It always requires faith to give the first. That's why so few Christians experience the blessings of tithing. It means giving to God before you see if you're going to have enough. By tithing, it is as if we are saying to God, "I recognize You first. I am putting You first in my life, and I trust You to take care of the rest of the things in my life."

That's why tithing is so important. It is the primary way we acknowledge that God is first.

The first portion is the redemptive portion. In other words, when the first portion is given to God, the rest is redeemed. In the same way, coming to church at the first of the week is a way of giving the Lord the first of your time.

Sadly, some people view Monday as the beginning of their week. They think, *I have to get this week started right. I have to put some deals together and get some money in the bank.* Thus, they give the first part of their week to money.

Other people think their week begins on Friday. They say, "Man, this weekend I'm really going to party and have a good time." These people give the firstfruits of their time to recreation.

As God's people, we need to give the first part of our week to Jesus. The reason the New Testament church met on Sunday was because they were celebrating the resurrection of the Lord Jesus Christ. They gave the first of their time to God in worship.

THE FIRST OF THE FIRST

Not only does the firstborn belong to God but firstfruits belong to Him as well.

In Exodus 23, we read:

> The first of the firstfruits of your land you shall bring into the house of the Lord your God (v. 19).

This verse goes even further and says it's the *first* of your firstfruits that God wants. That means the last of your firstfruits isn't acceptable. It's not the *tenth* portion of your firstfruits; it's the *first* portion of your firstfruits. Read that verse again:

The first of the firstfruits of your land you shall bring into the house of the Lord your God.

Notice that the Scripture designates "the house of the Lord" as the proper place to give firstfruits. It doesn't say to give them to a television ministry, although I believe strongly in supporting worthy media ministries. It doesn't say to give the first of your firstfruits to a missionary, even though supporting missionary work is near and dear to God's heart (and mine!). It doesn't say to give the first of your firstfruits wherever you want. It says to bring them "into the house of the Lord your God."

We must always give to the Lord's house first. This is an aspect of the principle of firstfruits that we need to understand. That's why Proverbs 3 says:

Honor the Lord with your possessions, and with the firstfruits of all your increase; so your barns will be filled with plenty, and your vats will overflow with new wine (vv. 9–10).

As this passage suggests, tithing to the Lord's house involves honoring the Lord with our possessions and with the firstfruits of all of our increase.

Now, in Old Testament times, most people were farmers. They raised animals and grew crops for their living. "Increase" came as crops were harvested and livestock reproduced. Today, you might be a banker or a lawyer or a teacher or a construction worker. Your increase comes in that way.

No matter how it comes, the Word makes it clear that we are to honor the Lord with the firstfruits of all of our increase. When we do, according to these verses, our "barns will be filled with plenty, and [our] vats will overflow" (v. 10).

Do you remember the account of the fall of Jericho in the book of Joshua? You'll recall that the Lord gave strict instructions that the Israelites were not to keep any of the spoils from Jericho. All of it belonged to Him, the Lord declared.

Why did the Lord say that all of the silver and gold from Jericho had to be given to the Lord's house? Because it was the *first* city conquered in the Promised Land. It was the firstfruits.

God was saying, "Bring all the silver and the gold from Jericho into My house, and then you can have all of the rest." He didn't say, "Conquer 10 cities and give Me all the spoils from the tenth one." He essentially said, "Give Me the first and you can have the rest." That took faith, of course—and so does tithing.

You'll also remember that one person among the Israelites disregarded God's clear instructions. The Israelites were told that the silver and gold were consecrated to the Lord (see Joshua 6:19), but a man named Achan took some for himself and became "accursed" (Joshua 6:18).

Think about that. When the spoils were given to God, they were "consecrated" or set apart for God's house; but after a man took some for himself, it was actually cursing Israel's efforts to take the Promised Land.

Consecrated or cursed—that's exactly what the tithe is all through the Bible. The tithe is consecrated to the Lord and for the Lord's house. But if we take it for ourselves, it becomes a curse because it's stolen.

In Malachi 3, God makes it clear that if we keep the tithe to ourselves, we are robbing God. What a sobering thing it is to consider that one can steal from God and, therefore, be under a curse.

> Will a man rob God? Yet you have robbed Me! But you say, "In what way have we robbed You?" In tithes and offerings. You are cursed with a curse, for you have robbed Me, even this whole nation (Malachi 3:8-9).

It is amazing to me how many people try to overlook this Scripture or explain it away. Some say, "Well, that's in the Old Testament." But in the very same chapter of Malachi, God says, "For I am the Lord, I do not change" (v. 6).

We have already seen that the Lord clearly says that the firstborn belongs to Him (see Exodus 13:2) and the firstfruits are His (see Exodus 23:19). We also just heard Him say that the tithe belongs to Him (see Malachi 3:8-9).

Here is my question to those who contend that the principle of the tithe is no longer active: If God declares, "I do not change" (Malachi 3:6), then when did those things supposedly change? When did God change?

The tithe, the firstborn, and the firstfruits all belong to the Lord. This isn't a law! It's an unchanging principle established by an unchanging God.

Many people say, "Well, tithing was under the law, so I don't have to do it. We're under grace now." They need to know that there are many things that were under the law that continue to be principles with God.

Would you believe anyone who asserted that because adultery was forbidden under the law, it is now acceptable under grace? Would you accept an argument that stated that because stealing was forbidden under the Old Testament law, it is now acceptable under New Covenant grace? Of course not.

There are eternal principles throughout the Word of God, and tithing is clearly one of them. It is a principle that runs from Genesis to Revelation.

The tithe belongs to God. The firstborn belongs to God. And firstfruits belong to God.

Throughout my life as an evangelist and pastor, I have been amazed at the consistency of the testimonies I hear about tithing. In more than 20 years of ministry, every tither I have spoken with has given me a similar testimony; every nontither has also given me a similar testimony, but one that is different from those who tithe. (And keep in mind the biblical exhortation to let everything be established by the mouth of two or three witnesses [see 2 Corinthians 13:1].)

Would you believe anyone who asserted that because adultery was forbidden under the law, it is now acceptable under grace?

Without exception, tithers say, "I'm blessed" or "God has blessed me." They all give the testimony that God is blessing them. In contrast, every nontither I have ever spoken with gives this testimony: "I can't afford to tithe."

Now I want you to think about these two statements and the two types of people they come from: All tithers give the testimony that they are blessed, and all nontithers give the testimony that they can't afford to tithe.

I think Forrest Gump could discern the pattern on this one. He would probably say, "I'm not a smart man, but I'm going to tithe. And that's all I have to say about that."

RESPECT FOR ABEL

The principles of tithing, the firstborn, and firstfruits are biblical and eternal. Aligning your life and actions with them can't help but bring God's blessing.

We find a great example of this in the Genesis 4:

> And in the process of time it came to pass that Cain brought an offering of the fruit of the ground to the Lord. Abel also brought of the first-born of his flock and of their fat. And the Lord respected Abel and his offering, but He did not respect Cain and his offering. And Cain was very angry, and his countenance fell (vv. 3-5).

Many people have wondered for years, Why did God respect Abel's offering but not Cain and his offering? The Word makes it a point to tell us very clearly that the offering Abel brought was the firstborn of his flock. But it doesn't say that Cain brought of the firstfruits of his crops.

Notice that the passage quoted above says, "and in the process of time." In other words, Cain grew his crops and then, "in the process of time," got around to bringing an offering to the Lord. The implication is that he didn't bring his firstfruits to the Lord. Could that be why God did not respect Cain's offering? I believe so.

Abel, on the other hand, brought the firstborn of his flock to the Lord, and God accepted his offering.

There is a lesson in this for us. God is looking at our hearts when we give. And when we give of the first of our firstfruits or our tithe, God receives and respects that offering. The tithe is your firstfruit. The tithe must be first! The Bible is clear on this matter:

> And all the tithe of the land, whether of the seed of the land or of the
> fruit of the tree, is the Lord's. It is holy to the Lord (Leviticus 27:30).

Just as the firstborn and the firstfruits belong to God, so does the tithe belong to Him. But like the other two, it must be *first*. As he declared, "all the tithe of the land ... is the Lord's" (Leviticus 27:30).

I once heard Mike Hayes, pastor of Covenant Church in Carrollton, Texas, use an excellent illustration of this truth.

Now, if I had 10 one-dollar bills to give away and asked two specific questions about them, I suspect most Christians would get the first one right but would scratch their heads at the second one.

Imagine, I've given you 10 one-dollar bills and have laid them out on a table in front of you. Now, my first question is, "How much is the tithe on this money?" I think everyone would get that one right. The tithe on *ten* dollars is, obviously, *one* dollar. But here's the more difficult question. Which *one* is the tithe? "Obviously, the first one," you might say. But *which one* is the first one? Is it the one on your left or is it the one on your right?

Let's say you get paid on Thursday and immediately pay all your bills, then buy groceries, and then go online to send your tithe. Have you tithed the first of your increase? No. Is it possible to give a full 10 percent and still not be tithing in accordance with God's principle? Absolutely.

For understanding, let's go back to the one-dollar bills. Which dollar is the tithe? Let me tell you how to decide that. The tithe is the first one spent or given. The first money you spend represents your firstfruits.

Is it really an act of faith to give 10 percent after all your other bills are paid? What does it say about our priorities when we willingly pay everybody else first and then see if there is enough left to give God His portion?

The first portion we spend should be the tithe. That is the firstfruit. And according to Exodus 13, that first portion is the redemptive portion. The first portion has the power to redeem the rest. This is the essence of Paul's message in Romans 11:16:

> For if the firstfruit is holy, the lump is also holy; and if the root is holy,
> so are the branches.

There are so many blessings that go along with tithing, but it is the principle of putting God first and the principle of faith that initiates the blessings. It is the trigger.

The first portion is the portion that redeems the rest. The first portion carries the blessing. That's why you don't want to give the first portion to the mortgage company. Unfortunately, it seems that many Christians fear the IRS and the mortgage company more than they fear God.

Another way to say that is, we respect them more than we respect the Lord. The tither says, "Yes, I have a stack of bills here, but I'm going to give to God first and trust Him to bless the rest of the 'lump.'"

There was much more at stake than money when Abraham offered his firstborn son, Isaac. You'll notice that Abraham didn't wait to see if he had 10 sons before he gave his first one. Nor did God go to Abraham when he only had Isaac and say, "After you have had four or five more sons, I'm going to come to you and ask you for one of them."

No, God asked for the first when one was all he had! Abraham had only the promise of having more sons. It took faith for Abraham to offer Isaac. And faith is precisely what tithing requires. It is giving God the first, in faith.

When God asked for the firstborn lamb, you had to give it in faith, with only the promise and hope that the ewe would produce more. Many people *say* they're putting God first, but true tithing is where the rubber meets the road. It is where we walk what we talk.

If you tell me that God is first in your life, then let me see your bank account. Then we'll really see who's first in your life. Will it say the mortgage company is first in your life? Does it say the car company takes a higher place on your list of priorities? Or is it the clear testimony of your spending patterns that God is first?

When Satan comes against you with fear and says, "You're going to go broke, your marriage is going to fail, you're going to get a disease," you can firmly reply, "No, I'm a tither, and because I tithe, the Bible says that God will rebuke the devourer *for my sake*. Yes, for *my* sake! God is first in my life, and God is going to redeem and protect everything else in my life!"

Would you rather try to make it through life with 100 percent of your income—but all of it cursed? Or would you rather try to make it through life with 90 percent of your income and all of it blessed, redeemed, and protected by God?

It is apparently a question many Christians need to ask themselves. Recently I heard a pastor share some alarming statistics:

In 1998, the body of Christ around the world earned the equivalent of an estimated $15.2 trillion. The total amount given to all ministry-related causes, including churches, missions, etc., was $270 billion. If you do the math, you will discover that is only 1.8 percent.

My first thought when I heard these statistics was that the percentage was surely skewed lower by all the poor countries included. Then I heard the numbers for the United States alone.

The body of Christ in the United States earned an estimated $5.2 trillion in 1998, and the total amount given in the United States was $92 billion. The amount given is 1.7 percent of the amount earned.

God doesn't need you to give— you need to be blessed.

Think about it. God's people in the United States, as blessed with abundance as we are, gave only 1.7 percent of our incomes to the cause of Christ. Yet the figure for the whole world was 1.8 percent. We are giving less than the poor countries of the world![1]

Please keep in mind, I'm not proclaiming the truth about tithing because God needs money; I'm delivering these truths for *your* sake. God doesn't need you to give—you need to be blessed.

My heart is broken for the body of Christ because of our lack of understanding of these principles and our failure to walk in God's blessings. My heart breaks because much of the body of Christ is living under a curse as a direct result of stealing from God. I counsel people all the time who are struggling, having conflict in their marriages and strife in their homes for this very reason. They don't understand that the firstborn, the firstfruits, and the tithe belong to God.

In 1 Corinthians 16, we read:

> Now concerning the collection for the saints, as I have given orders to the churches of Galatia, so you must do also: On the first day of the week let each one of you lay something aside, storing up as he may prosper, that there be no collections when I come (vv. 1–2).

Paul is telling us we should give every week, on the first day of the week, as we prosper. (*The New Living Translation* says, "In relation to what you have earned.") In other words, we should give to God in direct proportion to the size of our paychecks.

Notice that Paul began by saying for no collections to be taken when he comes (see v. 2). In other words: no special offerings. I long to see the day when we don't have to have candy sales in the foyers of our churches or Saturday car washes, because every member of the church is tithing.

Of course, the reason churches have so many special offerings is that only 1.7 percent of our income is being given to God.

Imagine what God's people could accomplish on the earth if His people faithfully gave Him the first 10 percent so that the remaining 90 percent is redeemed and blessed! Imagine the plans and purposes of God that could be advanced in this world if the Church would wake up to the blessings that come as a result of having the faith to give the firstfruits!

Oh, if only God's people would put Him first in their lives!

PASS DOWN THE PRINCIPLE

I want to end this chapter where it began—in Exodus 13. We started with a look at verses 12 and 13. Now let's examine the next two verses of that important passage:

> So it shall be, when your son asks you in time to come, saying, "What is this?" that you shall say to him, "By strength of hand the Lord brought us out of Egypt, out of the house of bondage. And it came to pass, when Pharaoh was stubborn about letting us go, that the Lord killed all the firstborn in the land of Egypt, both the firstborn of man and the firstborn of beast. Therefore I sacrifice to the Lord all males that open the womb, but all the firstborn of my sons I redeem" (vv. 14–15).

Here God is instructing the Israelites on how to pass down the principle of the firstborn to future generations. He is saying, "When your child asks, 'Why are we sacrificing this firstborn lamb, Daddy?' you are to sit him or her down on your knee and say, 'Let me tell you about when we were in Egypt. Let me show you the scars on my back. Let me describe to you what it's like to be a slave. We were in bondage. We were slaves, but God delivered us with a mighty hand. Because He set us free, this is the sacred covenant that we have made with God—to keep Him first in our lives. That's why we gladly give Him the first of all our increase.'"

I can tell you that I have had the New Covenant version of this happen with my own family.

At some time or another in the lives of each of my children, they have come to me when I was writing out the tithe check and asked me if they could be the one to give the check in the offering that day. Invariably, when I would give them the tithe check, they would look at the amount and say something like, "Wow! That's a huge amount of money, Dad. Why do we give this much to the church?"

And to each child I've been able to say, "You see, Daddy wasn't always a Christian. I didn't come to know Christ until I was 19 years old, and before I met Him, my life was a total wreck. Let me describe to you what it was like being in bondage—a slave to sin—but God delivered me with a mighty hand. That's why I gladly give God the first of everything He blesses us with—not out of duty or compulsion. No, I gladly give my tithe to God because I want to let Him know that He is first in my life. And because we give our first to the Lord, He blesses us, protects us, and provides for us."

We must live out these truths, and we must pass them down to our children.

A life of blessing begins with a clear understanding and acceptance of the principle of the firstborn, firstfruits, and the tithe. Without that understanding, it is impossible to move on to the greater adventures God has in store for those who will put Him first.

03

LIFE,
NOT LAW

Tithing is life, not law.

I feel the need to make that statement right up front because of the strong dose of truth I presented in the previous chapter. Over the years, I've had too many well-meaning but misguided Christians react to the message about tithing by telling me they don't tithe because "tithing is part of 'the law.'"

With all my heart, I want you to understand something: Tithing is not law to me—*it is life!*

Let me say that again. I don't tithe because tithing was a part of the Old Testament law; I tithe because it's life to me and to my family. Moreover, as we began to see in the previous chapter, it is a principle that runs throughout the Word of God. In fact, we saw that it predates the law of Moses by thousands of years.

The principle of the tithe (or firstfruits or firstborn) was in operation as Abraham was asked to offer Isaac and when he gave a tenth of the spoils to Melchizedek—a representation of Jesus Christ (see Genesis 14:18-20; Hebrews 5-7).

This principle goes all the way back to the opening chapters of Genesis, where we see Abel's offering accepted and Cain's rejected. In a sense, it even goes back further than that! We can see the principle of the tithe in God's instructions to Adam and Eve about the trees in the Garden of Eden.

Then the Lord God took the man and put him in the garden of Eden to tend and keep it. And the Lord God commanded the man, saying, "Of every tree of the garden you may freely eat; but of the tree of the knowledge of good and evil you shall not eat, for in the day that you eat of it you shall surely die" (Genesis 2:15-17).

Notice that in giving Adam and Eve stewardship of the Garden, God gave them every tree from which they could eat freely except for one. Exercising faithful stewardship of the Garden meant leaving that one tree alone. They were not to take that fruit for themselves and consume it. Being faithful stewards meant *life* to Adam and Eve. By choosing to eat of the fruit of the tree, they were acting like *owners* rather than *stewards*.

If something was right *under the law,* is it now wrong *under grace?*

Isn't that precisely how the principle of the tithe operates for us? God gives us stewardship responsibility over our lives. Though it *all* belongs to Him, He richly gives us all things to enjoy (see 1 Timothy 6:17). But He has asked us not to touch the firstfruits. "The tithe and the firstfruits are mine," says the Lord.

We demonstrate faithful stewardship—we show God that we realize that we are stewards, not owners—when we give Him the tithe.

As each of the previous examples shows, the tithe completely transcends the Old Testament law. But that shouldn't surprise us, because so do many other eternal principles.

Imagine what you would think if one evening you invited me over to your house for dinner and as I was walking out the door after a great meal, I grabbed your television and took it home. What if when you asked, "Why did you do that? The Bible says you're not supposed to steal," my response was, "Well, 'Thou shalt not steal' was part of the law. I'm not under the law. I'm under grace."

I am using a rather absurd illustration to make an important point. Just because something was mentioned in the law of Moses doesn't mean that we can throw it out now.

Let me address this issue in another way. If something was *wrong* under the law, can it be *right* under grace? In other words, since stealing was wrong under the law, is it now right under grace? Of course not.

Now let me turn the question around. If something was *right* under the law, is it now *wrong* under grace? Specifically, tithing was clearly the right thing to do under the law. The Old Testament makes that clear. But is it now the wrong thing to do under grace? Certainly not.

We can't afford to throw out any vital principles in the Word of God—and tithing is a principle that runs all through Scripture.

What most Christians fail to comprehend is that tithing is a test.

PASSING THE TEST

In Matthew 6, we find the familiar words, "For where your treasure is, there your heart will be also" (v. 21).

I want you to notice that it doesn't say where your heart is, there your treasure will be also (even though many people quote and apply it as if it did). It basically says that your heart follows your treasure. That is why tithing represents a test for every Christian. Keep reading and you'll see what I mean.

The word translated "tithe" in the Bible literally means "tenth"[1] or "a tenth part."[2] And do you know what the number 10 represents all through the Bible? It represents *testing*.

Let me give you a few examples. How many plagues were there in Egypt? In other words, how many times did God test Pharaoh's heart? The answer is 10.

How many commandments are there? In other words, in how many ways is our obedience tested? The answer is 10.

How many times did God test Israel while they were wandering in the wilderness? And how many times did God test Jacob's heart (by allowing his wages to be changed) when he was working for Laban? Or how many days was Daniel tested in the first chapter of the book of Daniel? In each case, the answer is, of course, 10.

> *The tithe represents the ultimate "heart test" for the believer.*

The pattern continues in the New Testament. In Matthew 25, 10 virgins had their preparedness tested. Ten days of testing are mentioned in Revelation 2:10. And, of course, Jesus had 10 disciples. (Actually, He had 12, but I was just testing you!)

What *is* true is that the number 10 is associated with testing throughout the Bible. And the tithe represents the ultimate "heart test" for the believer. But, more significantly, tithing is also the only area in which the Christian is invited to test God:

> "Bring the whole tithe into the storehouse, that there may be food in my house. *Test me in this,*" says the Lord Almighty, "and see if I will not throw open the floodgates of heaven and pour out so much blessing that you will not have room enough for it" (Malachi 3:10, NIV, emphasis added).

I remember having a conversation with God about this passage. I said something like, "God, why did You put those verses in the Old Testament? I mean, they only missed the New Testament by just a page or two. Why couldn't You have waited and put those verses in the New Testament? Didn't You know that everybody would try to explain these away because they are in the Old Testament?"

To that question, I felt as if the Lord spoke to my heart and answered, "I put those verses exactly where I wanted them. You see, tithing is a test of the heart. If I had put them in the New Testament, it wouldn't be as much of a test as it must be." Then, the Lord said, "However, I did put verse 6 in there for you."

At that point, I remembered what the Lord says in Malachi 3:6. As I pointed out in the previous chapter, in this verse He says, "For I am the Lord, I do not change."

Tithing truly is a test. The truth of this passage seems so simple to me. If I tithe, I'm blessed; if I don't, I'm cursed. Hmmm, that's a tough decision. Let me think about that. Tithe—I'm blessed. Don't tithe—I'm cursed. Blessings? Or curses? For me, that one really isn't that hard to figure out.

Still unsure about this tithing business? Then take God up on the offer He makes in Malachi 3:10. Test Him on it!

> "Bring the whole tithe into the storehouse, that there may be food in my house. *Test me in this,*" says the Lord Almighty, "and see if I will not throw open the floodgates of heaven and pour out so much blessing that you will not have room enough for it" (Malachi 3:10, NIV, emphasis added).

God is essentially saying, "Test me in this, I dare you, I double-dog dare you!" (Excuse my East Texas paraphrasing.) But clearly, God is saying, "Test Me."

That's why I want to extend a friendly challenge to you. Do the test! Begin to honor the Lord diligently with your firstfruits—the tithe—and see what happens.

OBEDIENCE AND THE CURSE

In response to this teaching, I have heard some people say, "This *curses* thing doesn't apply to me. As a believer, I can't experience any curses because Jesus bore the curse of the law for me on the cross." This does bring up an important issue. Let's examine it.

The Bible does clearly state that Jesus bore our sins, sicknesses, sorrows, pains, and shame on the cross. It is difficult to read Isaiah 53 without becoming overwhelmed with awe and gratitude for what Jesus did for us on the cross.

In Galatians 3, we also find a wonderful passage about the work of redemption that Jesus performed for us:

> Christ has redeemed us from the curse of the law, having become a curse for us (for it is written, "Cursed is everyone who hangs on a tree"), that the blessing of Abraham might come upon the Gentiles in Christ Jesus, that we might receive the promise of the Spirit through faith (vv. 13-14).

Without a doubt, Jesus bore all of these things—and more than we can imagine—on the cross. Now, let me ask you to consider something. As we just noted, Jesus bore your sin on the cross. First Peter 2:24 says, "Who Himself bore our sins in His own body on the tree, that we, having died to sins, might live for righteousness—by whose stripes you were healed." But have you sinned *since* you became a believer?

I'm sure the answer to that is yes. So think about that. Even though Jesus bore your sins on the cross, you have, nevertheless, sinned since you believed.

In a similar vein, we have also noted that Jesus bore our sicknesses as well. That is wonderfully, gloriously true. Yet, have you ever been sick since you became a Christian? I know I have.

Even though Matthew 8:17 says, "That it might be fulfilled which was spoken by Isaiah the prophet saying, 'He Himself took our infirmities and bore our sicknesses,'" we still battle the curse of sickness from time to time.

We must all appropriate, by faith, what Jesus did for us on the cross. And when we don't, we continue to experience some of the effects of the curse.

As believers, if we disobey the Word of God, we can still experience the effects of the curse. That applies to our finances just as surely as it does to our physical bodies. Can we, if we are in willful violation of God's principles of firstfruits, see our finances come under a curse? Yes, we can.

The good news is that we have the wonderful promise of Malachi 3, in which God promises to "rebuke the devourer" (v. 11) on our behalf if only we will dare to trust Him and obey.

LAW AND GRACE

As I have noted previously in this chapter, a common excuse for failing to tithe is, "I'm under grace, not the law."

The grace of God really is amazing. Yet, far too few Christians truly understand what grace is or how it operates. For one thing, the righteousness of grace always exceeds the righteousness of the law. This is the essence of what Jesus said in Matthew 5:

> Do not think that I came to destroy the law or the Prophets. I did not come to destroy but to fulfill. For assuredly, I say to you, till heaven and earth pass away, one jot or one tittle will by no means pass from the law till all is fulfilled. Whoever therefore breaks one of the least of these commandments, and teaches men so, shall be called least in the kingdom of heaven; but whoever does and teaches them, he shall be called great in the kingdom of heaven. For I say to you, that *unless your righteousness exceeds the righteousness of the scribes and Pharisees, you will by no means enter the kingdom of heaven* (vv. 17–20, emphasis added).

In this passage, we see an important truth—the righteousness of grace *always* exceeds the righteousness of the law. Notice that each time Jesus points to an Old Covenant law, He then sets a higher standard under New Covenant grace.

For example, the law said not to commit murder (see Exodus 20:13; Deuteronomy 5:17), but Jesus said not even to be angry with your brother (see Matthew 5:22). A higher standard! The law said not to commit adultery (see Exodus 20:14; Deuteronomy 5:18), but Jesus said not even to look at a woman lustfully (see Matthew 5:28). Once again, a higher standard.

In other words, the righteousness that grace demands (and Jesus *is* grace) goes further than that which the law demands.

That's why I smile when someone says to me, "I don't tithe because I'm not under the law. I'm under grace." I respond by saying, "Oh, so you give according to grace?" "Yes, that's right." Then I say, "Great! That means you give much more than 10 percent, because the righteousness of grace always exceeds the righteousness of the law. It's a higher standard."

The point is that there are certain principles that permeate the Word of God, and tithing is one of them.

Yes, when we give according to grace, we will give more than the tithe, but we *start* with tithing. The first 10 percent should be given as a firstfruits offering because it is a bedrock principle in the Word of God.

I suspect many believers think that the only Scripture on tithing is the one we read earlier in Malachi. Let me show you just a few of the other places in the Word where the principle of the tithe is established.

ABRAHAM, MELCHIZEDEK, AND YOU

In Genesis 14, we find a passage I have already mentioned:

> Then Melchizedek king of Salem brought out bread and wine; he was
> the priest of God Most High. And he blessed him and said: "Blessed be
> Abram of God Most High, possessor of heaven and earth; and blessed
> be God Most High, who has delivered your enemies into your hand."
> And he gave him a tithe of all (vv. 18–20).

A full 430 years before tithing was a part of the Mosaic law, Abraham tithed to
Melchizedek. According to the book of Galatians, Abraham is our spiritual father
and Melchizedek is a type of Jesus Christ (some prominent Bible teachers think
he might even have been Jesus Christ Himself!). Melchizedek's titles were "king of
righteousness" and "king of peace"—and, of course, Jesus is the true King of righteousness and peace.

We also know that Melchizedek is a type of Christ because the Bible explicitly
says so. In Hebrews 5, the inspired writer says of Jesus:

> And having been perfected, He became the author of eternal salva-
> tion to all who obey Him, called by God as High Priest *"according to
> the order of Melchizedek"* (vv. 9–10, emphasis added).

Likewise, the entire seventh chapter of Hebrews is devoted to showing how Jesus
is the fulfillment of all the types and shadows embodied in Melchizedek. It gives
particular attention to the fact that Abraham tithed to Melchizedek.

> For this Melchizedek, king of Salem, priest of the Most High God, who
> met Abraham returning from the slaughter of the kings and blessed
> him, *to whom also Abraham gave a tenth part of all*, first being translated
> "king of righteousness," and then also king of Salem, meaning "king of
> peace," without father, without mother, without genealogy, having
> neither beginning of days nor end of life, but made like the Son of God,
> remains a priest continually (vv. 1–3, emphasis added).

So Abraham, our spiritual father, tithed to Melchizedek, who was either Jesus Christ
Himself or a symbolic representation of Christ. Moreover, all this occurred 430
years before the law.

There is one other important thing mentioned later in this passage that I want
you to see.

> Here mortal men receive tithes, but there he [Jesus] receives them,
> of whom it is witnessed that he lives (Hebrews 7:8).

According to this remarkable verse, Jesus receives tithes in heaven. When you return your tithe, you may think you're giving it to your local church, but in a very real, spiritual sense, true tithers have their offerings received by the Lord Jesus Himself.

What a privilege! What a holy thing! And what a loss for those who never take the step of faith and tithe.

A HEART THING

Let's look at another passage in which the principle of the tithe is evident.

In Genesis 28, we find the patriarch Jacob having his famous encounter with God in a dream, with a rock as his pillow. His life and heart having been changed, he rises and says:

> And this stone which I have set as a pillar shall be God's house, *and of all that You give me I will surely give a tenth to You* (v. 22, emphasis added).

Jacob's vow to tithe came straight from his grateful heart. That's what I want you to see. True tithing comes from the heart—not from a legalistic mind. I also want you to note that this promise came 400 years before the law.

Like his grandfather Abraham, Jacob wanted to give God the first of his first-fruits—the first 10 percent. Having experienced the sweetness of God's presence and the goodness of His favor, Jacob wanted to bless Him. It was a heart thing.

That's why tithing is life to me, not law. And when it becomes life to you, it will be one of the greatest joys of your life.

We see another insight into the power of tithing in Leviticus 27. We find God giving instructions to the Israelites about how to prosper in the land of promise:

> And all the tithe of the land, whether of the seed of the land or of the fruit of the tree, is the Lord's. It is holy to the Lord (v. 30).

God considers the tithe holy. The word "holy" means "separated" and "set apart."[3] In other words, the first 10 percent is to be separated and set apart for the Lord. It is not for me to determine what to do with it. It is God's tithe.

In Deuteronomy 26, God says:

> And it shall be, when you come into the land which the Lord your God is giving you as an inheritance, and you possess it and dwell in it, that you shall take some of the first of all the produce of the ground, which you shall bring from your land that the Lord your God is giving you, and put it in a basket and go to the place where the Lord your God chooses to make His name abide (vv. 1-2).

A little further down in this chapter, God says:

> Then you shall say before the Lord your God: "I have removed the
> holy tithe from my house, and also have given them to the Levite, the
> stranger, the fatherless, and the widow, according to all Your command-
> ments which You have commanded me; I have not transgressed Your
> commandments, nor have I forgotten them. I have not eaten any of
> it when in mourning, nor have I removed any of it for an unclean use,
> nor given any of it for the dead. I have obeyed the voice of the Lord
> my God, and have done according to all that You have commanded
> me" (vv. 13–14).

Notice the key phrase, "I have removed the holy tithe from my house."

When you understand that the tithe is holy, you don't want it in your house. You want to get it to the house of God where it belongs. You don't use part of it for your vacation. You don't use it to pay for your children's school tuition. You know that holy means set apart.

THESE YOU OUGHT TO HAVE DONE

The New Testament isn't silent about the principle of the tithe either. In fact, Jesus made a very plain statement on the subject in Matthew 23:

> Woe to you, scribes and Pharisees, hypocrites! For you pay tithe of
> mint and anise and cummin, and have neglected the weightier mat-
> ters of the law: justice and mercy and faith. These you ought to have
> done, without leaving the others undone (v. 23).

Jesus is obviously scolding the Pharisees here. He points out that they are meticulous about tithing, but that they have "neglected the weightier matters of the law."

But I want you to notice what He says at the end of this stinging indictment. He declares, "These [meticulous tithing] you ought to have done, without leaving the others undone." In other words, He says to them, "Yes, tithe of all your increase, but don't neglect the vitally important heart issues of justice, mercy, and faith."

Think about it. What we just read is, in my opinion, one of the most amazing Scriptures on tithing. Jesus Himself affirmed the tithe. I don't know how anyone with a soft heart toward God could get around this.

Of course, tithing isn't a grim duty. It isn't a dry religious exercise. And it isn't a punishment. It is an amazing opportunity that brings tremendous benefits to the tither. We see this in action in 2 Chronicles. This is a long passage about a decree of King Hezekiah, but it is worth the time it takes to read:

Moreover he commanded the people who dwelt in Jerusalem to contribute support for the priests and the Levites, that they might devote themselves to the law of the Lord. As soon as the commandment was circulated, the children of Israel brought in abundance the firstfruits of grain and wine, oil and honey, and of all the produce of the field; *and they brought in abundantly the tithe of everything.* And the children of Israel and Judah, who dwelt in the cities of Judah, brought the tithe of oxen and sheep; also the tithe of holy things which were consecrated to the Lord their God they laid in heaps. In the third month they began laying them in heaps, and they finished in the seventh month. And when Hezekiah and the leaders came and saw the heaps, they blessed the Lord and His people Israel. Then Hezekiah questioned the priests and the Levites concerning the heaps. And Azariah the chief priest, from the house of Zadok, answered him and said, "Since the people began to bring the offerings into the house of the Lord, we have had enough to eat and have plenty left, *for the Lord has blessed His people*; and what is left is this great abundance" (31:4-10, emphasis added).

The gist of this passage is this: When God's people began to tithe, God began to bless them even more. The more they were blessed, the larger their tithes grew. This upward cycle of blessing and abundance resulted in heaps of goods and food in God's house.

When Hezekiah came and saw the heaps, he basically said, "Explain this to me; are the people doing okay? They have given so much!" And the priests said something like, "You need to understand something, King. Since the people began to tithe, God has blessed them. What you see here is the tithe of the abundance with which God has blessed them."

Can you imagine what the body of Christ could accomplish if every believer tithed?

This passage illustrates the two parallel results of tithing. It blesses God's people, but it also brings provision into God's house. Remember what God said in Malachi: "Bring all the tithes into the storehouse, that there may be food in *My house*" (3:10, emphasis added). King Hezekiah commanded the people to bring in the tithe so that the priests might devote themselves to studying the Word of God.

Can you imagine what the body of Christ could accomplish if every believer tithed? What kind of impact the Church could have on our culture and on cultures around the world if the heaps would begin to accumulate in our houses of worship? How much more effective could your pastor be if he had a support staff that liberated him to devote his time to the Word and prayer?

I am so blessed and grateful to pastor a congregation of people who have embraced God's life-giving truth about tithing. As the senior pastor, I see my main responsibility as leading and feeding the congregation. As a result, I spend most of my time studying, praying, and seeking the Lord.

Why am I able to do so? Because I have a gifted executive senior pastor who takes care of all the details of church administration and management. Because we have so many tithers, we also are able to provide numerous other pastors and ministers with specialized areas of responsibility.

In contrast, most pastors have to do everything themselves because the resources to hire support staff simply aren't available. They have to do all of the hospital visitation, all the counseling, and all the administration of the church business.

These pastors are still expected to bring fresh, relevant, powerful sermons each Sunday. They are still expected to be God's man of anointing and power.

Oh, how I wish every pastor had the time and the staff that I have so that they could spend more time with the Lord. This will happen as God's people come to understand the power of tithing and the benefits they will receive when their pastors are able to study, pray, and bring them messages from the throne room of God every week.

CARING FOR GOD'S BRIDE

Finally, our perspective on tithing will change when we begin to see the local church as a visible manifestation of God's Bride.

Consider this illustration:

> I have to go on an extended journey, and I choose three men for a special responsibility. I say to those three men, "I'm going to send you each $10,000 every month. You may keep $9,000 of the money and spend it as you please. But I want you to give $1,000 each month to my wife for the meeting of her needs."
>
> As promised, I send each of these men $10,000 monthly. After a few months, I call my wife and ask her if she is receiving the support I had arranged. Her reply is, "Well, the first one is sending $1,000 each month, just as you instructed him. The second one is actually sending $2,000 a month. I don't know why, but he is. But the third

one sent $800 the first month, $300 the second month, and nothing the third month."

Now, as a husband who loves his wife with all his heart, what do you think I'm going to do? I am the one providing the money to these men. I've told them they can keep $9,000 for themselves. All I wanted them to do was give a mere 10 percent so that there could be food in my house! (see Malachi 3:10).

Well, with the first man who was being faithful to follow my instructions, I am going to continue sending him that $10,000. But for the third man—the one who wasn't satisfied with the 90 percent I graciously gave him—I am going to quit sending him $10,000 a month and send it to the most generous man instead. Why? Because I can trust the second man. He has demonstrated that he cares about what I care about. He is a good steward.

What the third man was doing was the same as stealing from me. (Remember the verse, "Will a man rob God? Yet you have robbed Me! But you say, 'In what way have we robbed You?' In tithes and offerings" [Malachi 3:8].)

Now let me bring this illustration home. Jesus has gone away for a season of time. He has said to each of us, "I want you to take care of My Bride (the Church) while I am away by giving 10 percent to My house. You can spend the remaining 90 percent as you desire."

Those who obey will be blessed. Those who go above and beyond will be blessed even more. But from those who refuse to do even the minimum, He's going to take what they have and give it to someone who will be a good steward with it.

Matthew 25:29 says, "For to everyone who has, more will be given, and he will have abundance; but from him who does not have, even what he has will be taken away." The rewards of good stewardship are great.

God doesn't change. Tithing remains an extraordinary opportunity for blessing and abundance for those with the faith to trust Him.

It is also the foundation upon which all the other principles I'm about to share with you are built. The blessed life awaits you. However, it begins with a heart commitment to honor, obey, and bless the Lord with your tithe.

THE PRINCIPLE
OF MULTIPLICATION

Have you ever wished you could multiply your money? Well, I have wonderful news for you: God is able to do it.

Of course, that shouldn't come as a surprise to us. He multiplied oil and meal for a poor widow and her son. He multiplied the strength of outnumbered Israelite soldiers in battle after battle. And He multiplied fish and loaves on a couple of Galilean hillsides. Clearly, God is a Master of multiplication.

In Luke 9, we find the account of one of those miraculous multiplications—the feeding of the 5,000:

> When the day began to wear away, the twelve came and said to Him, "Send the multitude away, that they may go into the surrounding towns and country, and lodge and get provisions; for we are in a deserted place here." But He said to them, "You give them something to eat." And they said, "We have no more than five loaves and two fish, unless we go and buy food for all these people." For there were about five thousand men. Then He said to His disciples, "Make them sit down in groups of fifty." And they did so, and made them all sit down. Then He took the five loaves and the two fish, and looking up to heaven, He blessed and broke them, and gave them to the disciples to set before

the multitude. So they all ate and were filled, and twelve baskets of
the leftover fragments were taken up by them (vv. 12–17).

You are probably very familiar with this story, but let's modernize and personalize it a bit. You may see some things you have never noticed before.

Put yourself in the place of the disciples. See yourself as one of the Twelve—you're basically a member of the official Messiah search committee. That means you're trying to determine whether or not Jesus is the true Messiah. You've left your fishing boats and begun traveling with Him on a nationwide speaking tour.

One day, an enormous crowd gathers. You are very excited because this is the most people ever to attend one of these traveling seminars. Counting the heads of households, you come up with a figure of about 5,000 men plus women and children. That means there are probably 15,000 to 20,000 people gathered on the hillsides listening to Jesus. (You are amazed at how far a voice can carry from the tops of these hills.)

He preaches all morning, and you expect Him to wrap up around noon (the time everyone is used to getting out of church so that they can get to the cafeteria ahead of the Essenes and the Sadducees). But He doesn't. He keeps right on teaching.

You think, *Well, He's preaching well and everyone seems to be enjoying it. We'll let Him go a little bit longer today.* Then 12:30 pm comes and goes, and He is still preaching. One o'clock, two o'clock, three o'clock, and four o'clock all come and go, and still the prophet continues expounding on the Scriptures!

By five o'clock, you are beginning to hear from your associates. "The people are hungry, and all the restaurants are going to close soon!" The fact is, you're not sure whether it's really the people who are hungry or just your associates. But, being pretty famished yourself, you go to Jesus.

"Lord, please excuse the interruption, but uh … some of the other disciples and I were starting to, uh … You know … get concerned about the people. … You know how people are. I mean, uh … they haven't eaten all day, and now the restaurants are going to close. So, we were thinking that You might want to … You know, uh … dismiss the service."

And so the Lord turns to you and matter-of-factly says, "*You* give them something to eat," then returns to His teaching.

You let the implications of His words sink in. There are 15,000 to 20,000 hungry people scattered across those hillsides, and the Lord tells *you* to give them something to eat.

So, you go back to the committee. "Did you tell Him that the people were hungry?" they ask. You nod. "Did you tell Him that He needs to dismiss the service?" You nod again.

"Well, is He going to dismiss the service?"

"Not exactly," you tell them sheepishly.

"Not exactly? What does that mean? Didn't you tell Him that the people need to eat?!"

"Yes."

"And what did He say?"

"He said *we* should give them something to eat."

"Come again? For a minute there, I thought you said *we* were supposed to give them something to eat."

"That's what the Master said."

So, you all fan out to see how much food you can scrounge up. Thirty minutes later, you meet back up and take inventory.

"Let's see," you announce to the committee, "altogether, we have ... two fish sticks, five hushpuppies, a Long John Silver's kid's meal sack, and a SpongeBob SquarePants action figure. Perfect!"

You, of course, draw the short straw, so you have to report back to Jesus. "Excuse me, Lord. Sorry to interrupt You again," and you go on to give Him the exciting news about your food collection efforts. *Now, surely, He will dismiss the service*, you say to yourself. (Looking nervously at your watch, you try to calculate how fast you'll have to walk in order to make it to the Bethsaida Pizza Hut before it closes.)

Then Jesus looks at you, smiles, and says, "That's great! Have the people sit down in groups of 50." Stunned, you head back to the committee.

"Is He going to dismiss the service?" they ask when they see you coming. They're sounding a little irritable. *Low blood sugar*, you think.

"No."

"No?!"

"He wants us to have the people sit in groups of 50."

"Didn't you tell Him that all we have to feed 20,000 people is a Long John Silver's kid's meal?"

"Yep. Groups of 50."

What follows would be funny if you weren't so hungry and exasperated. Have you ever watched 12 guys try to organize 20,000 men, women, and children into groups of 50? Herding cats across Texas would be a breeze by comparison.

Ultimately, you and the committee have everyone grouped as instructed (that's the first miracle of the afternoon).

As you return to Jesus, you can't help but try to figure out how He's going to provide for this group. (That's the tendency for all of us. We want to figure out in advance how God is going to provide for our needs. We're usually wrong.)

At that point, Jesus takes the fish and hushpuppies, looks up toward heaven, and blesses them.

TWO KEYS TO MULTIPLICATION

I have taken some creative liberties with this story in hopes of encouraging you to put yourself in the shoes of the disciples that day. I want you to see, in your mind's eye, what happened out there on that hillside.

After He blessed the food, Jesus began breaking it in half and handing it to the disciples. Can you imagine what someone like Peter was thinking as he looked down at that half piece of bread? He had handed Jesus a whole piece and only got back half!

I just wonder if Peter, looking down at that little fragment, might have said to the Lord, "Uh, are You sure You're through praying? Wouldn't You like to pray a little more?" The Lord might have said, "No, I've blessed it. Now go give it away."

Peter walked away with that half piece of bread in His hand and, obediently, broke it in half the same way he had seen Jesus do. Handing out chunks of bread, he broke it in half again and again and again. This is what we've missed in this remarkable story. The miracle didn't happen in the Master's hands—it happened in the disciples' hands. You know the outcome. With each of the disciples duplicating this pattern, the result was 12 big baskets of leftovers.

> *Something must be blessed*
> *before it can multiply. In other words,*
> *it has to be given to the Lord first.*

Embodied in this real-life account, there are two very important principles for us. They are the two keys to multiplication in the kingdom of God.

The first principle is this: Something must be blessed before it can multiply. What many Christians fail to understand is that before your money can multiply, it has to be blessed. In other words, it has to be given to the Lord first.

As we have seen in previous chapters, when we give the first of our increase, the tithe, to the Lord, the rest of it is blessed. Remember the words of Romans 11:

> For if the firstfruit is holy, the lump is also holy; and if the root is holy,
> so are the branches (v. 16).

I know many sweet Christians who have never seen their finances multiply. And often the reason is that the money hasn't been blessed. When you give it to the

Lord first and the Lord puts His blessing on it, then, and only then, does it have the ability to multiply.

Jesus, the One who receives our tithes, is the only One who has the power to bless it so that it can multiply. That's the first principle of multiplication.

There is a second principle of multiplication: Only what is given away can multiply.

In the example we were just exploring, the disciples had the bread and the fish. It had been blessed, and so it had the potential to multiply. But if they had just eaten it themselves, it would have remained five loaves and two fish. It would never have multiplied. They would have had a couple of bites of food each instead of full stomachs and 12 baskets of leftovers. They had to give it away so that it could multiply.

This is another thing I have observed in those who have said to me, "I've never seen my finances multiply." Sometimes those who are tithing give little or nothing over and above the tithe. They don't realize that only that which is given away can multiply. "But isn't tithing a form of giving?" you may be asking.

Tithing isn't really giving—it's returning.

I believe there is a difference between tithing and giving. I believe that tithing is simply returning to God that which He has said is His. Giving our firstfruits, our first 10 percent to the Lord via a local church, is what causes that which is ours to be blessed.

You can't give that which doesn't really belong to you. The firstfruits are the Lord's. The rest is yours to keep or give as you choose. It is from this account that you give what the Bible often refers to as offerings.

Tithing isn't really giving—it's returning. It is bringing back to the Lord what is already His. Thus, the second principle of multiplication is that finances over and above the tithe must be shared if they are to multiply.

THE POWER OF OFFERINGS

In Matthew 25, Jesus tells a story of three stewards. One steward was entrusted with five talents. When accounting time came around, he returned those five talents to the Lord, plus five more. And the Lord said, "Well done, good and faithful servant" (v. 21).

There was another steward who was entrusted with two talents, and, likewise, he returned to the Lord more than He had given him.

But then there is the third steward—the one who was entrusted with one talent. He said to the Lord, "There you have what is yours" (v. 25). He only returned to the Lord what was already His. And the Lord called him a wicked and lazy servant.

Now, please don't misunderstand me. I'm not suggesting that anyone who only tithes is wicked and lazy. I am saying, however, that there is a principle of faithful stewardship that teaches that we should give more to God than just the tithe because tithing is simply returning to Him what is already His.

If you're not currently tithing, that is certainly the place to start. Tithing is where we remove the curse. Tithing is what brings the blessing on the balance of our finances. Tithing is what causes God to rebuke the devourer and open the windows of heaven. It is the foundation on which our giving is built.

But if you look closely at Malachi 3, God mentions more than the tithe there. He mentions "tithes and offerings" (v. 8).

In other words, it's tithes *and* offerings that remove the curse. It's tithes *and* offerings that bring the blessings. It's tithes *and* offerings that rebuke the devourer.

I'm convinced that God wants to bless and multiply our finances—just as He blessed and multiplied the two fish and the five loaves.

The truth is that God can cause our finances to go further than we could ever cause them to go through our own cleverness or diligence. I know this is true, because I've seen it operate in my own life over and over.

God wants your finances to be blessed, and He wants your finances to be multiplied. But it is vital to understand that you will never see the multiplication of your finances until you understand these two principles:

1. We give to the Lord first so that our finances are blessed.

2. We give over and above our tithes because only that which is shared can be multiplied.

These are the principles of multiplication. And they are as powerful today as they were on that Galilean hillside.

BREAKING THE
SPIRIT OF MAMMON

In less politically correct times, before all things remotely Christian were purged from public schools, many high school students were required to read John Milton's epic poem *Paradise Lost*.

If you were one of them, you know this poem painted a pretty detailed portrait of hell. In it, Milton showed Satan as a fallen commander in chief surrounded by his demon generals. Among them are Moloch, Dagon, Astarte, Osiris, and Belial.

Each of these, of course, was the god of an idol-worshipping culture in ancient times and is mentioned in the Bible. But Milton's poem depicts another demon standing at Satan's side. That demon's name is Mammon.

You may recognize "mammon" as a New Testament word. Jesus mentions it in a couple of places. For example in Matthew 6, Jesus declares:

> No one can serve two masters; for either he will hate the one and love the other, or else he will be loyal to the one and despise the other. You cannot serve God and mammon (v. 24).

After reading this verse, you can see why Milton would lump a demon named Mammon in with all those Old Testament idols. Jesus clearly suggests that it is *possible* to serve mammon instead of serving God, but He goes even further: Jesus states it is *impossible* to serve both at the same time.

He says that you will love the one and hate the other. You will be loyal to one and despise the other. According to Jesus, there is no middle ground—no half-and-half. Mammon, apparently, is a jealous god.

Jesus certainly makes a striking contrast between the Spirit of God and the spirit of mammon. But just what is mammon?

"Mammon" is an Aramaic word that essentially means "riches."[1] And, apparently, the Assyrians got the concept of a god of wealth from their neighbors, the Babylonians.

Babylon was a city founded on pride and arrogance (remember the account of the tower of Babel in Genesis 11). At its heart is an attitude that says: Man doesn't need God. We're self-sufficient. This is what the spirit of mammon tries to tell us: You don't need God. Trust in riches!

In the biblical sense of the word, mammon is the spirit that rests on money. Did you know that all money has a spirit on it? It either has the Spirit of God on it or the spirit of mammon.

Money that is submitted to God and His purposes has the Spirit of God on it—which is why it multiplies and cannot be consumed by the devourer. I'm convinced that money that has been submitted to God—wealth that is devoted to serving Him rather than trying to replace Him—is blessed by God. In a very real sense, God's Spirit blesses it.

On the other hand, money that is not submitted to God has the spirit of mammon on it by default. That's why people so often try to use money to control or manipulate others. It's why people think money can bring them happiness or fulfillment.

Mammon is basically the spirit of the world—and that spirit is a liar.

THE RULE OF MAMMON

I have noticed that the people most under the influence of the spirit of mammon tend to have the most fear about their money.

That's why Jesus said, "You cannot serve God and mammon" (Matthew 6:24). Mammon wants to rule. The spirit of mammon is looking for servants. It is seeking worshippers. It will promise you everything but deliver nothing.

As Jesus clearly suggests, mammon tries to take the very place of God. Pastor Jimmy Evans, senior pastor of Trinity Fellowship Church in Amarillo, Texas, said, "Mammon promises us those things that only God can give—security, significance, identity, independence, power, and freedom. Mammon tells us that it can insulate us from life's problems and that money is the answer to every situation."[2]

When you think about it, mammon is nothing more than the system of this fallen world that stands in sharp opposition to God and His ways. For example, mammon says to buy and sell; God says to sow and reap. Mammon says to cheat and steal; God says to give and receive. But more than anything, mammon wants to rule.

It's no coincidence that in the book of Revelation, the Antichrist attempts to dominate people through the use of economics—preventing people from buying or selling unless they submit to him (see 13:17). In this way, the brief rule of the Antichrist will be through the spirit of mammon.

It's no wonder Jesus said you cannot serve both God and mammon. Why? Because the spirit of mammon stands in direct opposition to the Spirit of God.

Now, don't get the wrong idea—money and mammon are not synonymous. Money is not inherently evil. One of the most frequently misquoted verses in all of the Bible is in 1 Timothy 6:

> For the love of money is a root of all kinds of evil (v. 10).

Notice, the Bible doesn't say that money is the root of all kinds of evil. It says that *the love of* [or the worship of] money is a root of all kinds of evil. It is the idolatrous love of the spirit of mammon that is evil. In other words, greed, covetousness, and selfishness are all manifestations of the spirit of mammon.

The reason we cannot serve both God and mammon is that the spirit of mammon is the opposite of the Spirit of God. Mammon says to take; God says to give. Mammon is selfish; God is generous. And so on.

Mammon is a spirit and, as such, talks to us all the time. Mammon says, "If you have the right credit cards, the right clothes and the right car, and you live in the right neighborhood and know the right people, you'll be happy and fulfilled."

Mammon tells you that if you had more money, people would listen to you, your relationship problems would go away, and life would be sweet—you could do what you want, go where you want and live the way you want.

Money is not the answer to problems—God is.

Sadly, people in the world aren't the only ones susceptible to this kind of deception. Mammon sometimes engages in creative lying to ensnare Christians as well. The spirit of mammon can get religious when it has to. For example, sometimes mammon says, "If you just had more money, you could really start helping people." (Keep in mind, Jesus never told anyone the answer was more money. Money is not the answer to problems—God is.)

Many times, when we're under pressure, the thought will come to us (and it's actually mammon speaking to us) that we need one of two things to happen: We either need God to miraculously change our circumstances or we need someone to drop a truckload of money on us. This daydream usually involves winning the lottery, a contest or sweepstakes, or the death of a wealthy relative we didn't know about.

Notice how the spirit of mammon tries to position itself as a substitute for God. "You either need God to work a miracle right now or you need more money." That's simply a lie. We need God, period.

This is precisely why I am very cautious of multilevel business opportunities. I have been invited many times to meetings where these opportunities are shared. I am usually invited because someone has observed my God-given ability to communicate, and he or she wants to harness that gift for building the business. Of course, I'm not going to do that. God has given me this gift to get lost people saved and to teach His people His Word.

On the occasions I have attended these meetings, I have seen the spirit of mammon working in very subtle ways where Christians are concerned. Often, the pitch is this: If you were rich, just think of all the people you could help; or, your church or favorite ministry will have everything it needs after you become a millionaire!

My friend, God can help people without money. When we start thinking that most of our problems can be solved by having more money, it's a sign we're under the influence of the spirit of mammon.

Don't misunderstand. Jesus is not telling us to hate money. He is saying that if we love God, we will hate mammon—the greedy, selfish, lying, deceiving, Antichrist-like spirit that operates through money worship.

As Jesus proclaimed, either we will love one and hate the other or we will be loyal to one and despise the other (see Matthew 6:24). We are to despise the spirit of mammon that lies to people, promises everything but delivers nothing, and dares to try to take the place of God.

Both God and mammon are always talking to us. Every time we're praying about giving sacrificially to our local church or to a ministry, mammon is there whispering to us (or occasionally shouting).

TRUE RICHES

There is a longer passage in the New Testament in which Jesus talks about choosing between God and mammon. Here is the passage from Luke 16:

> And I say to you, make friends for yourselves by unrighteous mammon, that when you fail, they may receive you into an everlasting home. He who is faithful in what is least is faithful also in much; and he who is

unjust in what is least is unjust also in much. Therefore if you have not been faithful in the unrighteous mammon, who will commit to your trust the true riches? And if you have not been faithful in what is another man's, who will give you what is your own? No servant can serve two masters; for either he will hate the one and love the other, or else he will be loyal to the one and despise the other. You cannot serve God and mammon (vv. 9-13).

Here Jesus calls mammon unrighteous, but note that He wasn't calling *money* unrighteous. Mammon and money aren't synonymous. Jesus was calling the spirit that can rest on money unrighteous.

Money can be used for either unrighteous or righteous purposes. It can be used for temporal or eternal purposes. Money that has been submitted to God (as opposed to being used in an attempt to replace Him) is blessed. And that's why blessed money multiplies and is not consumed by the devourer. It's money that can be used for good and to bless others.

What else does this passage tell us? It says that we are to use our money for that which is eternal. And what in our lives is eternal? People! The only lasting things you will encounter today are people. The human soul is eternal.

If I use my money to bring people to Christ, they will welcome me into heaven when I die. Use your money to affect people—to help them hear the gospel—and they will form part of your welcoming committee when you get to heaven.

Notice, Jesus doesn't say that *money* will welcome you. He says that the friends you make will receive you into an everlasting home. I know one day I am going to be greeted by people who are in heaven because I gave to churches, ministries, and missionaries that are bringing people to Christ.

Just as He turned water into wine, God can turn money into souls. He is the only One who can transform unrighteous mammon into true riches.

In a similar vein, in Matthew 6, Jesus says:

Do not lay up for yourselves treasures on earth, where moth and rust destroy and where thieves break in and steal; but lay up for yourselves treasures in heaven, where neither moth nor rust destroys and where thieves do not break in and steal. For where your treasure is, there your heart will be also (vv. 19-21).

When we use money for righteous purposes, we are laying up treasure in heaven. That's why I want to be a wise steward of money. I want to use it to invest in churches and ministries that are investing in people. I want my money to be used in helping people, loving people, feeding people, and caring for people.

This is one of the reasons, as a family and as a church, we give consistently to James Robison's ministry, Life Outreach International. It is a ministry that is affecting people in powerful and positive ways—both physically and spiritually. At this writing, the ministry feeds and clothes more than 400,000 hungry children each month around the world. They also share Christ with them, and of course, the people listen because they have seen a tangible demonstration of God's love in the form of lifesaving aid.

I know that one day in heaven some people from Africa are going to greet me and say, "I'm in the kingdom because you supported Life Outreach International. Thank you for letting God turn unrighteous mammon into heavenly treasure."

This is why I keep emphasizing that money is not inherently evil. God uses money to feed and clothe people. He uses it to facilitate and spread the gospel to the unreached parts of the earth.

This explains why the enemy of our souls works so hard to corrupt and distort our thoughts about money. The devil knows that God can take temporal money and turn it into eternal souls. He knows that the more money we give to the church, the more souls are going to be saved, the more the kingdom of God is going to be advanced, and the kingdom of darkness is going to fail.

Hell is being plundered by our offerings, and Satan knows it! The devil hates Spirit-led giving because it simultaneously diminishes his kingdom and makes us more like our heavenly Father.

That's why I stated in the opening words of the introduction that the devil doesn't want you to read this book. He doesn't want you to get free financially; therefore, he doesn't want you to tithe and give offerings so that your money can be blessed and multiplied.

It is not how much we have that matters— it is whose *it is.*

At this point, you might be thinking, *Well, to be honest, I don't have enough of this "unrighteous mammon" to make any of this relevant to me. I don't need to know about stewardship and giving because I don't have any money!*

To that, I would lovingly but frankly say, "And you never will if you don't embrace this principle." In verse 10 of the passage we previously read, Jesus says:

> He who is faithful in what is least is faithful also in much; and he who is unjust in what is least is unjust also in much (Luke 16).

The Bible says that we must be faithful with a little before we will be entrusted with much. If you have just a little bit of money, you are a perfect candidate for blessing because if you will be faithful with that little, God will give you more.

God is looking for people He can entrust with much. He also knows that a person who is unjust with a little will be unjust with more as well. Christians who will cheat with a little won't suddenly become faithful if they are given a lot. That is why Jesus says:

> Therefore if you have not been faithful in the unrighteous mammon, who will commit to your trust the true riches? And if you have not been faithful in what is another man's, who will give you what is your own? (Luke 16:11–12).

What I'm trying to help us see is that it is not how much we have that matters—it is *whose* it is. If we belong to God, then it's His money, not ours.

That is why Jesus tells me I need to be faithful with what is someone else's. It's not mine; it's His. And each new day brings a test of my stewardship.

A COMPLETE TRANSFORMATION

I must tell you that I grew up a very selfish, proud, and materialistic individual. My parents were certainly not that way. They are, and always have been, great givers. To this day, they help people buy houses that they could not afford on their own.

My mother and father are both very, very generous people. But for whatever reason, I was quite materialistic as I was growing up.

But when, at the age of 19, I got saved, the first thing I wanted to do was give. I wanted to give to everyone I could. I wanted to bless others and help them know what I had found.

When God finally got hold of me and changed my heart, my wife and I had a combined gross income of about $600 per month. In those early days, we had a budget that would allow us to go out to eat one time per month.

I distinctly remember the first time we ever went out to eat after I had accepted Christ. I found myself wanting somehow to share Jesus with the waitress who was serving us. Then an idea came to me. If I didn't order a meal, I could take that money and leave it as an extra generous tip along with an evangelistic tract. Maybe the tip would encourage her to read the tract and come to know the Lord. So that's what we did. Before we left, we said a few words to her about how much God cared about her.

About a month later, we were back in that restaurant for our monthly "splurge." Through the month, I had prayed that God would bless us with enough extra money to be able to leave an even bigger tip along with another tract.

Just as I had asked, our faithful God had allowed us to accumulate an extra $50 that we could leave along with a booklet about salvation. That night we requested that same waitress and left her a $50 tip on a $10 meal.

We returned to the restaurant one month later, very eager to see if that waitress was still working there. She was, indeed.

When she saw us, she said, "I read that little booklet you left last time you were here." We tried not to show how excited we were to hear that. She continued, "And I prayed that prayer to receive Christ at the end of it." Of course, we were thrilled to hear that. But she wasn't finished. "Then I called my husband on the phone and read the whole booklet to him, and he prayed that prayer too."

At that point, I said, "That's wonderful! But what do you mean, you called your husband? Does he travel for a living?"

Looking embarrassed, she said, "No, my husband is in prison. He will get out in two or three years. We both want to thank you for leaving me that booklet and being so generous. Money has been pretty scarce since he went to prison."

Over the next few years, my wife and I discipled this sweet waitress and saw great spiritual growth. We also began to mentor her husband in prison. When he was released, he joined the church with his wife, and they were baptized together. I had the privilege of knowing that the lives and eternal destinies of this couple had been changed because I gave.

And I gave because Christ had changed my life.

EXPERIENCING THE BLESSING

I mentioned earlier that when Debbie and I got married, our combined gross income was $600 per month. That is an annual income of $7,200.

After a few months of tithing and giving extravagantly to the Lord, Debbie got a different job that paid $18,000 per year. About that same time, I began preaching and doing revivals. That first year, my income from offerings was $32,000. Thus, together, our annual income went from $7,200 to $50,000.

In our second year of marriage, as we continued to tithe and give whenever and wherever the Holy Spirit directed, Debbie quit her job in order to stay at home while my income increased to $72,000. Our income had now risen from $7,200 to $72,000—a tenfold increase.

Within three years, our income had risen to more than $100,000, and by God's grace, we were giving 70 percent of it away (and having the time of our lives doing it!).

There is something significant to God about tenfold and hundredfold returns. I've seen it throughout my whole life. (Remember the story I related in chapter 1 about the man at the pizza place who gave me 10 times the amount I had just given away to the missionary?)

I remember one occasion in which I was at a ministry conference in the large Dallas Convention Center arena. We were sitting way up in one of the balcony sections toward the back of a crowd numbering around 10,000. We didn't have very much money at that point, but at offering time, I felt strongly that the Lord wanted me to give $100. It was going to be a step of faith to give that amount.

The minister who was receiving the offering said, "I want you to pray and ask God to bless the offering you're giving." When he said that, I felt impressed to hold the offering up over my head as we prayed. Just as I did, a thought came to me, so I just prayed it. I said, "Lord, I ask You for a hundredfold return of this offering so that I can give even more to the kingdom of God."

I didn't know it at the time, but there was a man sitting on the arena floor up near the platform. At the moment I lifted my offering to the Lord with a heart full of gratitude, God spoke to him and told him to turn around and look. As he turned around, he noticed, way back in the upper reaches of that arena, the tiny figure of a man with his hands raised to the Lord. The Spirit of God spoke to him and said, "I want you to go give that man $10,000."

Later, the man found me and gave me a check for $10,000—exactly 100 times the amount I had just given.

Please understand what I'm saying. The money is not the point. It's the joy that we receive from giving. It's the power that comes from obedience. I'm not presenting giving as a get-rich-quick scheme. On the contrary, I'm presenting it as a lay-down-your-life challenge.

But as we give, God blesses. And the greatest blessing of all is being able to see God's kingdom enlarge, to see ministries advance, to see churches grow and to see broken people become whole—all because of our obedience in giving.

That's what I'm excited about. It's what I want you to understand. I was lost and without hope. I didn't know Christ. Jesus gave His all to save an arrogant, prideful nobody. So I can do no less than give my all for Him.

God speaks to us about our money, and so does the spirit of mammon. Who is your master? To whom are you listening?

MAMMON HAS FRIENDS

Over the years, I have observed a couple of other spirits that tend to run in the same circles, especially when it comes to wealth and giving. Just as a spirit of mammon will keep you from living the blessed life, so will a spirit of poverty or a spirit of pride.

A spirit of poverty will cause you to be ashamed of the blessings of God. If you are a faithful, generous steward, you *will* be blessed. There is no avoiding it. As we have seen over and over in this book, the more you give away, the more God bestows.

Being a giver *will* result in blessings. The devil can't stop it, but he can try to make you ashamed of it. This is the job of the spirit of poverty, and I've seen it afflict both the poor and the wealthy. In fact, it is more common in the rich than in any other group! It manifests itself as a sense of shame and guilt about being blessed by God. Think about this for a moment: Is there anything God could do in your life for which you should feel ashamed? Of course not. However, by simply doing things God's way, many believers receive blessings and somehow feel as if they have to apologize for them. Don't ever do that. Don't ever allow the enemy to make you ashamed of God's blessings.

Now, if you're not susceptible to the trap of a poverty mentality, the enemy will try the opposite approach—a spirit of pride. Pride says, "You've earned this stuff. Your hard work, ingenuity, and talent have made it happen. Thus, you should be *proud* of the blessings you have received."

These spirits work from opposite ends of the spectrum but have a common root—they get us to focus on "stuff" rather than God. We become centered on the blessing rather than on the Blessor.

The spirit of pride says, "Wealth comes from hard work." The spirit of poverty says, "Wealth comes from the devil." The spirit of pride says, "You should be proud of what you have." The spirit of poverty says, "You should be ashamed of what you have." They are both traps because they are things-focused rather than God-focused.

Let me give you some real-world examples of how these spirits manifest themselves so that you can discern their attacks in your life.

How do you respond when someone compliments you on your watch or your outfit? Pride says, "It's imported from Europe." Poverty says, "This old thing? I got it at Target."

The spirit of pride tries to make people think we paid more for things than we did. The spirit of poverty wants people to think we paid less. Poverty feels the need to justify purchases and possessions because it equates blessing with evil. It causes you to say, "I can't let you think I spent very much money on anything because that would mean I'm not spiritual."

Do you see the trap?

EXPOSING A POVERTY MENTALITY

Let me say it again: If you have been blessed by God because you've done things His way, stop feeling guilty. Don't be ashamed of having a heart God can bless!

I speak from experience here. There was a time in which God had to show me just how prevalent the poverty mentality was in my thinking. It was especially strong because I have been in the ministry all my adult life (and everyone knows that preachers are supposed to be poor).

I remember purchasing a very nice jacket once and then returning it because I felt guilty about wearing it. It was a golf jacket that was just what I had wanted and needed for some time. I found it at a golf shop at half price. I called Debbie from the pro shop to get her opinion, and she said, "It's a great deal. Buy it!"

I wore it directly out onto the golf course and proceeded to play some of the worst golf of my life. Of course, the spirit of poverty was quick to place the blame for my horrible score on the new jacket. *God didn't want you to have the nice jacket. You've missed God, and now your golf game is cursed!*

Believe it or not, as soon as the round was over, I returned the jacket and got my money back. But that wasn't the end of it. In the days that followed, I began to grieve over "having" to return that jacket. I stewed about it, and I actually found myself resenting God. *I can't believe I can't even have a nice jacket. Other people get to have nice things, and I can't even buy a coat without my golf game being cursed. It's not fair, God!*

After putting up with this nonsense for about three days, God eventually got my attention and spoke very clearly, "Quit blaming Me for your not having that jacket! I didn't tell you to take that jacket back."

Then He said something I've never forgotten. The Lord said, "Son, I never speak to you through guilt or condemnation." He also added, "And, by the way, don't blame Me for your lousy golf game. You've never needed any help from Me to play badly."

God not only uses our stuff to test us, but He uses other people's stuff as well.

Isn't it amazing that so many of God's people feel as if they must explain away the presence of anything good or nice in their lives; or if anyone compliments them on something, they feel compelled to justify it?

My friend, you don't have to justify your purchases to anyone but God. If God gives you peace about buying something, don't worry about what anyone else thinks about it!

RIGHTLY RELATING TO THINGS

As I have pointed out previously, God uses things to test our hearts and reveal what's inside. The truth is that God not only uses *our* stuff to test us, but He uses other people's stuff as well. In other words, how we respond to someone else being blessed says a lot about the condition of our hearts.

It is no coincidence that the tenth commandment essentially says that you shall not covet your neighbor's stuff. The Greek word translated "covet" in the Bible is *epithumeo*, and it means "to set the heart upon."[3] It is very similar to the Greek word for "lust," which is *epithumia*.[4]

To covet something is to set your heart upon it. This is a problem, because we are to set our hearts upon nothing and no one but God. God doesn't care if we have stuff; He cares if stuff has us!

Have you noticed that in the movies all materialistic people are wealthy? But in real life, some of the most materialistic people don't have very much.

A person's net worth doesn't tell you anything about his heart. Some of the most materialistic people I have ever encountered were poor. By the same token, some of the most heavenly minded, sold-out-to-God, nonmaterialistic people I know are quite wealthy.

God wants us to go after *Him*. It is the theme of this book: *It's the heart that matters.*

SELF-EVALUATION

How can you know where your heart is? First, ask yourself these questions: Am I looking to God or to people to meet my needs? Do I get angry or resentful with people who don't help me as I want them to? Do I blame others for my circumstances?

These are all warning indicators of looking to men rather than to God as our source of provision. When people have been looking to men rather than God to meet their needs, they are ultimately disappointed. Then they become bitter.

We must also discern the presence of a spirit of pride or poverty in our lives. It is vital to our spiritual health and effectiveness in God's kingdom that those spirits be replaced by a heart of gratitude. Here are some tests to help you discern the difference:

> **When you think about your situation in life ...**
> Pride says, "I deserve more!"
> Poverty says, "I should feel guilty."
> Gratitude says, "Thank you!" (Gratitude is an attitude of thankfulness that always acknowledges God's provision.)
>
> **When someone says, "Wow, you have a nice house!"**
> Pride says, "We were going to build a bigger one."
> Poverty says, "It was a foreclosure."
> Gratitude says, "Thank you. The Lord has blessed us!"
>
> **When someone says, "That's a nice suit!"**
> Pride says, "It's tailor-made."

Poverty says, "It was half price."
Gratitude says, "Thank you!"

When someone says, "That's a nice car!"
Pride says, "I've got three of them!"
Poverty says, "It's a company car."
Gratitude says, "Thank you!"

Pride wants people to think that we paid more. Poverty wants people to think we paid less. Gratitude doesn't care what people think; it only cares what God thinks! How about just telling the truth? When someone remarks about something you exercise stewardship over, just tell the truth and be grateful.

THE COMPARISON TRAP

Pride causes us to compare ourselves with others. Poverty causes us to compare others with ourselves.

When someone pulls up beside you in a less expensive car, pride says, "Mine's better!" When someone pulls up beside you in a more expensive car, poverty says, "That's a waste! He's probably a crook."

Pride and poverty do have this in common—they both always get us to compare ourselves with others!

In sharp contrast, a person with a heart of gratitude compares himself with God and says, "Thank you!" Why? Because when I compare what I have done for God (which is nothing) with what God has done for me (which is everything), my heart naturally overflows with gratitude.

Don't fall into the comparison trap. Pride says, "I earned it." Poverty says, "I shouldn't have it." Gratitude says, "I received it by grace."

As we have seen, the key to resisting the spirits of mammon, pride, and poverty is to remember. We must remember that we were slaves to sin, the work God has done in us by grace, and that although we have worked hard, it has been God's blessing on our lives that has produced anything good.

This is the message God gave the Israelites before they entered the land of promise:

> And you shall *remember* the Lord your God, for it is He who gives you
> power to get wealth, that He may establish His covenant which He swore
> to your fathers, as it is this day (Deuteronomy 8:18, emphasis added).

If, as you have read this chapter, you have discerned signs of mammon, pride, or poverty in your life, you may want to pray a prayer like this:

> *Dear God, please forgive me for being selfish, prideful, and covetous. Please forgive me for listening to the unholy spirits of mammon, pride, and poverty. Lord, I ask you to break them off of me, off of my family, and off of my descendants. And help me, from this day forward, to be a generous, extravagant giver to the kingdom of God. In the name of Jesus. Amen.*

06

IT TAKES A HEART TRANSPLANT

I think Luke 6:38 is a wonderful verse of Scripture. But I'm also convinced it's one of the most frequently misapplied and misunderstood verses in the Bible. Its words are very familiar to most Christians. You can probably quote it from memory:

> Give, and it will be given to you: good measure, pressed down, shaken together, and running over will be put into your bosom. For with the same measure that you use, it will be measured back to you.

One of the most common mistakes people make about this verse is assuming that Jesus is speaking only of money. In truth, He's revealing a principle that applies to every area of our lives.

This becomes crystal clear if you look at the larger context of the verse. For instance, back up a couple of verses and look at 36 and 37:

> Therefore be merciful, just as your Father also is merciful. Judge not, and you shall not be judged. Condemn not, and you shall not be condemned. Forgive, and you will be forgiven.

It is only then that Jesus says, "Give, and it will be given to you" (v. 38). Yes, this principle applies to money, but you can also give forgiveness. You can give mercy. You can give understanding. You can give patience.

Jesus is simply talking about the broad principle of giving. Whatever you give is going to be given back to you in "good measure, pressed down, shaken together, and running over" (Luke 6:38).

To capture the full meaning of this truth, you need to know a little more about what the terms, "good measure," "pressed down," "shaken together" and "running over" refer to. In reality, these were farming terms.

According to instructions in the Old Testament, farmers in Israel were to leave the grain in the corners of their fields for the poor. Thus, each year at harvesttime, there were two sets of harvesters in the field: the primary harvesters in the middle of the field who were being paid to bring in the crop and the poor people in the corners who were harvesting the crop in order to feed themselves and their families.

Primary harvesters out in the middle of the field would fill up a basket then carry it over to the barn or wagon. They would then dump it out and go back to the field to begin filling the basket once again. To these workers, it didn't really matter how full their baskets were. They were being paid by the hour, so they didn't care. They just needed to stay busy and keep working until all the grain was in the barn.

This was not the case, however, for the poor people working in the corner of the field. That field was probably nowhere near their homes. They had probably walked several miles to get there. However much food they could get in their baskets would be the amount of food available to their families. They had life-and-death incentive to get as much into that basket as possible.

If you were in that position, you would first make sure you had put in a good measure—not just a partial measure or a half measure. Then you would press it down to compress the grains together to create more room. After topping the basket off again, you would then shake it to eliminate any air spaces between the grains. Having done all that, you would then pour in as much grain as you possibly could, heaping it up above the rim until it began to spill over the sides.

It is one thing to receive a basket of free grain. It is a far better thing to receive a good-measure, pressed-down, shaken together, and running-over basket of free grain.

That's why the Lord chose to use these terms. He knew His listeners in Israel would instantly connect with the point He was trying to make. What He communicated was that whatever you give, you're going to get a lot more of the same in return. This is a universal principle with God. You always receive back more than you give.

Think about it this way. When you give away an apple seed by planting it, you don't just get back an apple seed. In time, you actually get back a whole apple tree, and on that tree are many apples, and each apple has many seeds. You get back so much more than you actually give.

Yet this is precisely where so many people go wrong regarding this passage of Scripture. Once you understand the wonderful truth of it, there is a tremendous temptation to make it your *motivation* for giving.

Many well-meaning preachers and Bible teachers actually fall into this trap and thus encourage others to do the same. The "give and it shall be given to you" principle is to be our *reward*, not our motivation.

That's why Jesus preceded this promise by saying, "Judge not, and you shall not be judged. Condemn not, and you shall not be condemned. Forgive, and you will be forgiven" (Luke 6:37).

This context puts the promise in a very sobering light. If you give judgment, judgment will be given back to you, good measure, pressed down, shaken together, and running over. If you give condemnation, condemnation will be given back to you, good measure, pressed down, shaken together, and running over. It works both ways!

The good news is, if you give forgiveness, an abundance of forgiveness will be given back to you. If you sow love, you will receive an overflowing harvest of love.

This is a fundamental principle in the kingdom of God. It is a truth I have heard called the law of reciprocity. But approaching it in a balanced way is very much a matter of the heart.

The basic problem I have with most of the teaching I've heard on Luke 6:38 is that material gain is presented as the motive for giving. How do you think God feels when a preacher gets up and essentially says, "Come on! Give to God, and you'll get back more! This is a great deal!"?

> *How must God feel when His people only get excited about giving toward His kingdom purposes when they are whipped into a frenzy through get-rich-quick promises?*

As I have pointed out, it is true that you can't outgive God. The principle of reciprocity applies just as fully to money as it does to judgment and forgiveness. But there is nothing in Scripture that says we should make personal gain our motive for giving.

How must God feel when His people only get excited about giving toward His kingdom purposes when they are whipped into a frenzy through get-rich-quick promises? Do you think God ever says, "Boy, if only My people could catch the vision of having a lot more stuff"?

God doesn't want us to catch the vision of *getting*. He wants us to catch the vision of *giving*.

Yes, as we do, we will receive much more in return. And, no, God is not against our having nice things. On the contrary, He loves to see His people blessed. But motives are everything!

As Proverbs 16 tells us:

> All a man's ways seem innocent to him, *but motives are weighed by the Lord* (v. 2, NIV, emphasis added).

And James confronts the issue directly:

> When you ask, you do not receive, because you ask *with wrong motives,* that you may spend what you get on your pleasures (4:3, NIV, emphasis added).

When it comes to pleasing God and operating in line with His kingdom principles, heart motivation is what matters.

THE BIGGER PICTURE

We have discovered that if we back up a few verses from Luke 6:38, we begin to see its message in a little different light. Well, we get even more context and perspective if we back up a little further. Let's begin with verse 30:

> Give to everyone who asks of you. And from him who takes away your goods do not ask them back. And just as you want men to do to you, you also do to them likewise. But if you love those who love you, what credit is that to you? For even sinners love those who love them. And if you do good to those who do good to you, what credit is that to you? For even sinners do the same. And if you lend to those from whom you hope to receive back, what credit is that to you? For even sinners lend to sinners to receive as much back. But love your enemies, do good, and lend, hoping for nothing in return; and your reward will be great, and you will be sons of the Most High. For He is kind to the unthankful and evil (Luke 6:30–35).

Now we have the greater context of the familiar, "Give, and it will be given to you" (v. 38). Not coincidentally, this passage begins with the words, "Give to everyone who asks of you" (v. 30). Both verses, beginning with the word "give," can go a long way toward helping us catch the revelation of giving.

As I have suggested, the thing that bothers me about the way people have preached Luke 6:38 is with material gain presented as the motive for giving rather than a by-product of it.

The message of Jesus' sermon is *"Give!"* Give to those who ask of you. Give to those who can't pay you back. Give love to those who don't deserve it. Give mercy to those who wrong you. Give the kind of treatment you would hope to receive from others. Give, give, give! Oh, and by the way, when you do, your heavenly Father will make sure you get much more in return.

Do you see the subtle but important distinction in emphasis? When you give with what looks to the world like reckless abandon, you are following God's example.

He is kind to the unthankful and the evil (see v. 35)—that was you and me at one time. God extended ultimate kindness to us by sending His Son when we were unthankful and evil people.

God is a giver. And, yes, it's true that when we give, God will give back to us, but that should not be our motive for giving. We should give for the pure joy of imitating our wonderful Father.

It's our hearts the Lord is concerned about. And a properly focused heart is more excited about the giving part than the receiving part.

In other words, God is saying, "When you give just to give, I'm going to reward you by giving back to you in much greater measure." The reward comes because we have allowed God to do a work in our hearts in the area of giving—not in the area of getting.

There is an Old Testament glimpse of this truth in Deuteronomy 15. There God says:

> If there is among you a poor man of your brethren, within any of the gates in your land which the Lord your God is giving you, you shall not harden your heart nor shut your hand from your poor brother, but you shall open your hand wide to him and willingly lend him sufficient for his need, whatever he needs. Beware lest there be a wicked thought in your heart, saying, "The seventh year, the year of release, is at hand," and your eye be evil against your poor brother and you give him nothing, and he cry out to the Lord against you, and it become sin among you. You shall surely give to him, and *your heart should not be grieved when you give to him, because for this thing the Lord your God will bless you in all your works and in all to which you put your hand.* For the poor will never cease from the land; therefore I command you, saying, "You shall open your hand wide to your brother, to your poor and your needy, in your land." If your brother, a Hebrew man, or a Hebrew woman, is sold to you and serves you six years, then in the seventh year you shall let him go free from you. And when you send him away free from you, you shall not let him go away empty-handed; *you shall supply him liberally* from your flock, from your threshing floor,

and from your winepress. From what the Lord has blessed you with, you shall give to him. *You shall remember that you were a slave in the land of Egypt, and the Lord your God redeemed you;* therefore I command you this thing today (vv. 7–15, emphasis added).

Here is a clear view of God's heart for helping people. It is also more evidence that God looks at the heart attitude of the giver. He makes it a point to tell the Israelites not to let their hearts "be grieved" (v. 10) when they give. All the way back then, God loved a "cheerful giver" (2 Corinthians 9:7).

It's not hard to understand why this is so. Aren't you proud of your children when they are unselfish? Are you blessed when you have to bribe or threaten them to get them to be generous?

We're pleased when our children help and prefer one another in love. And what is true for us as earthly parents is infinitely true for God.

Furthermore, when we grow to become cheerful, willing givers, we become more and more like our heavenly Father. God is trying to do a work in us. He wants to purify our hearts.

But, as the passage we just read points out, there are some things about ourselves we are going to have to confront if we are to become pure-hearted givers.

THE SELFISH HEART

According to Deuteronomy 15:9, we're going to have to deal with the wicked thoughts that would keep us from having compassion for others. Here God clearly labels selfish thoughts as wicked. Selfishness whispers that we won't have enough or that God won't be faithful to meet our needs if we give. God says, "Don't allow your heart to think that way."

Obviously, greed and selfishness are not proper motives for giving. God wants to change us from greedy, selfish takers into grateful, generous givers.

In Joshua 1, we read:

This Book of the law shall not depart from your mouth, but you shall meditate in it day and night, that you may observe to do according to all that is written in it. For then you will make your way prosperous, and then you will have good success (v. 8).

Many people read that verse and come away thinking that the key to being prosperous and having good success is to meditate on the Word. Take another look and you'll see that they are only half right. This verse actually says that we are to meditate day and night on the Word so that we can *do* everything it says to do! It's *doing* the Word that brings success and blessing.

That's precisely why selfishness is your enemy. Selfishness tries to manipulate and make deals with God. We were born selfish.

At the risk of offending you if you're a brand-new parent, I must tell you that your precious angel sprang from the womb completely and utterly self-absorbed.

Every baby's first verbal expression isn't "mama" or "dada." It's "waaaaaah!," which can be roughly translated as, "Feed me! Change me! Hold me—now!"

And have you also noticed that the favorite word of every English-speaking two-year-old on the planet is "Mine!"?

Clearly, selfishness is deeply rooted in all of our hearts, and this doesn't change just because our bodies grow up. If you doubt this, just try helping yourself to a pork rib or chicken wing on a man's plate sometime. It's a good way to lose a hand. Perhaps you haven't noticed, but most men do not like to share food.

Most women, on the other hand, are happy to share their food. Watch a group of women at a restaurant and you'll witness more food swapping than you'll find in the commodities pit at the Chicago Mercantile Exchange. This explains why a woman assumes her man will be more than happy to share from his plate. She is wrong.

This dynamic plays out thousands of times each day in fast food drive-thrus across this great land of ours.

A husband and wife drive up to the menu speaker and hear, "Welcome to Burger Circus. May I take your order?" The husband leans out the window and, talking quite a bit louder than necessary, says, "Yeah, I'd like a double cheeseburger and some french fries and a coke."

He then turns to his wife and asks, "What would you like, dear?" And what does she say? "Oh, I don't want anything. I'll just have some of yours." *Some of mine*, the man thinks. *Doesn't she understand that "mine" is ... well ... mine? I ordered the amount of food that I wanted to eat!*

Of course, the man doesn't actually say any of this. Instead, he says sweetly, "Honey, if you want something, I'll order it for you. If you want some fries, I'll get you some fries." "No, no," she says, "I'm not really hungry." Of course, the husband knows that at least half of his fries are as good as gone.

My point is we are all selfish. The default condition of the human heart is to hoard and avoid sharing with anyone. Then a loving heavenly Father comes to us and says, "I want to deal with this wicked, selfish heart and make you a giver. I want to make you like Me."

THE GRIEVING HEART

"And your heart should not be grieved when you give to him."

That's what the Lord said in the passage we read from Deuteronomy 15. After addressing the fact that we have a selfish heart, the second thing we have to deal with when it comes to giving is a grieving heart.

Take a look at the whole verse:

> You shall surely give to him, and your heart should not be grieved when you give to him, because for this thing the Lord your God will bless you in all your works and in all to which you put your hand (v. 10).

Notice that the reward for being a giver is a blessed life. God says He will bless you in everything you put your hand to and in all your works.

But He instructs us not to grieve in our hearts after we have been obedient in giving. It's important not to let yourself start grieving over what you could have done with the money if you had kept it for yourself. Selfishness can attack us *before* we give, but grief can attack us *after* we give.

People who sell big-ticket items for a living know about something called buyer's remorse. The term refers to something that frequently happens to people who spend a lot of money on an item, such as a car or house. After the excitement of the moment wears off, they can experience a panicky what-have-I-done feeling. Many items purchased on impulse are returned the following day as a result of this phenomenon.

Many people give because they feel they have to rather than because they want to.

Something similar may happen when you have been obedient to give as the Holy Spirit prompts. That means you have to guard your heart not only before you give but afterward as well.

Here's another problem: Many people give because they feel they have to rather than because they want to. They feel *pressured* to give, and afterward they grieve over that gift. They grieve over the money they no longer have.

God is trying to do something deeper in our hearts. If we are filled with regret after being a blessing, does it please God? Has He accomplished the work in our hearts He wants to perform? Not at all.

So, how do you combat grief? You do it with a proper perspective regarding "your" money.

To illustrate this perspective, I once stopped right in the middle of a sermon and said, "You know what? I need someone to give me $100." Immediately, a man jumped up, came to the front, and handed me a one-hundred-dollar bill. I stuck the bill in my pocket and continued right on with my sermon.

I am sure every person in the congregation was thinking, *What was that all about? Why did he ask for $100? And why was that man so quick to get up and give him $100?* (I suspect the person who was thinking it the most was the man's wife!)

After letting everyone stew on it for several minutes, I interrupted my message once again to explain. "Let me tell you why that gentleman was so quick to bring me $100 without knowing why I needed it. Before the service, I gave him the one-hundred dollar bill and told him I would ask for it during the service. I asked him to bring it up quickly when I asked for it."

I went on to explain that I was trying to illustrate a point for them. The reason the man gave the money promptly when I asked for it was that it was mine in the first place. He experienced no grief, remorse, or emotional conflict about giving me the money. Why? Because he knew it wasn't his.

As we saw in a previous chapter, the same is true of everything we have. It is all God's, and we merely exercise stewardship over it. When we get God's perspective on money—when we understand that God owns it all—it is easy to give it when He asks for it. We give it to Him freely, and we don't grieve over it. We understand that it wasn't ours in the first place.

Whenever I observe a Christian operating selfishly, I know I'm looking at a person who either doesn't know or has forgotten that it all belongs to God. They are acting like an owner, not a steward.

The man who gave me the money during my sermon really didn't give it to me, did he? He simply returned it. Maybe we have a problem with giving because we don't understand stewardship. Perhaps we've forgotten that God is the owner, and that in sharing, we are actually just returning to God what is His in the first place.

So, let me ask you: Does your heart ever grieve over giving money? Do you ever find yourself feeling sorrow over money lost? You can stop it. It wasn't yours in the first place!

MORE HEART SURGERY

Beyond overcoming a selfish heart, beyond avoiding a grieving heart—there is a third heart adjustment that we must make in the area of giving. With God's help, we must develop a liberal or generous heart.

Now I am not using the term "liberal" in the political sense. I'm talking about liberality—the practice of being generous and free with our material possessions.

Look once again at this verse about giving to the poor from the passage in Deuteronomy 15:

You shall supply him liberally from your flock, from your threshing floor, and from your winepress. From what the Lord has blessed you with, you shall give to him (v. 14, emphasis added).

We may not have threshing floors or winepresses nowadays, but we are still called to give liberally from that which God has blessed us. We are not to be stingy in our giving; we are to be generous. That's why we must cultivate a liberal heart.

This goes against the grain of our fallen natures, but it is perfectly consistent with the new natures we received when we gave our lives to Jesus. Often I say, "I was born selfish, but I was born again generous."

The key to walking in the new nature, rather than the old one, is simply a matter of renewing the mind. "And do not be conformed to this world, but be transformed by the renewing of your mind" (Romans 12:2). Mind renewal brings transformation.

My new nature—the spirit man inside of me—wants to be generous, but I must learn to renew my mind in this area. I must come to trust that God will take care of me if I'm a generous giver.

My old nature used to try to figure out how I could manipulate circumstances in my favor. Of course, that's the attitude of a taker, not a giver. Selfishness tries to manipulate God or "make deals" with Him where giving is concerned. But a liberal-hearted person gives quickly and generously because he knows it all belongs to God, and he trusts in God to take care of him and bless him.

To no credit of my own, this is a work God has done in my heart. And I am writing this book to testify to you that it works. God *is* faithful.

Some time ago, Debbie was talking with a pastor and his wife who were staying in our home. They could clearly see that we were living the blessed life, so the pastor asked my wife, "Why do you think God has blessed you so much?"

Debbie thought about it a moment and answered, "I think it has to do with Robert's heart. When Robert got saved, God so changed his heart that he would give away everything we owned if he sensed God telling Him to do it. As a matter of fact, he's done it several times because he loves God and he loves people. The Lord has given him a heart that wants to give generously to God's people and God's work."

I can't begin to tell you how much joy giving has brought to our lives. Being givers in God's kingdom is the most fun we have ever had. It has resulted in a more exciting life than we could ever have imagined.

A FINAL WORK OF THE HEART

When we allow God to change us in this area, there is one more work He must do in our hearts. We have to develop a *grateful* heart.

Look back at Deuteronomy 15 one last time:

> You shall remember that you were a slave in the land of Egypt, and the Lord your God redeemed you; therefore I command you this thing today (v. 15).

Why did God instruct the Israelites to remember that they had been slaves? Because it would fill their hearts with gratitude for what He had done for them.

From time to time, in worship or in my quiet time, God reminds me of my past. He doesn't do it to produce guilt or condemnation. He knows it produces deep gratitude. I was such a mess. I was on a road of heartache and self-destruction, and then He saved me and put me on the road of life and blessing. When I think about that, my heart overflows with thankfulness.

When we allow God to remind us that we used to be slaves and that everything we have is by His gracious hand, it will help us to be grateful. And when we're grateful, we're generous. Genuine gratitude to God is a rare and powerful thing.

One time when I was preaching in a very small church on the subject of giving, a friend of mine, a liberal giver, came along to support me in prayer as I preached. He also was praying for the people who were hearing the message—that God would do a work in their hearts in the area of giving.

At the end of the message, I said, "I want each of you to pray and ask the Lord what He wants you to give tonight." At that point, as my friend began thinking about what God might want him to give, he realized he hadn't brought his wallet with him. To his dismay, he discovered that he had nothing at all to give in the offering.

He prayed, *Lord, what can I give? I don't have any money with me!* Immediately, the Lord reminded him that he had on a brand new pair of very expensive shoes. The Lord said, *I want you to give those shoes to the pastor of this church.*

The pastor of that little church would probably have never purchased such a nice pair of shoes for himself, even if he could have afforded them, which he probably could not.

At that point, my friend began going through all those mental gymnastics one goes through when God asks you to do something unusual. *What if they're not the right size? Will he be offended? What will people think? Am I just going to walk out of here in my socks?*

Finally, he made a decision, *The Lord has spoken to me, so I'm going to do it whether or not it makes sense.*

He went over to the pastor's wife and asked, "What size shoes does your husband wear?" It was the very same size he was wearing. Needless to say, my friend rode home with me in his stocking feet. But he was blessed and full of joy—and so was that pastor.

Several years later, I heard the story of a man who was in the congregation that very same night. He had just recently come to know Christ. Prior to being born again, he had squandered all of his money and was essentially broke. At offering time, he said, *Lord, what can I give? I have so little money, but my heart is so full of gratitude for what You have done for me.*

As he told it, the Lord gave him the idea of taking out a life insurance policy and making the church the beneficiary. So he arranged for a $100,000 policy. Just a few years later, he passed away, and the church received that money—a larger gift than he could possibly have given any other way.

GRATITUDE OR GREED

As I have said before, a heart of true gratitude is a rare and precious thing. Over the years, I have gotten a little glimpse of how God must feel as Debbie and I have been involved in blessing and giving to other people.

The fact is that any time we have ever given something to someone, we have encountered one of two attitudes. People respond to a blessing with either gratitude or greed. Let me explain what I mean.

This second response is most common when we have chosen to give to someone on several occasions. When you give to someone once, they may be surprised and grateful. But after you have been generous several times, there is a tendency for the person to start seeing the gift as an entitlement.

We respond to God in the same manner all the time. God repeatedly blesses and gives and, before long, it is *expected*. If it stops showing up, we are offended and mad.

It's greed or gratitude. I had an experience that beautifully illustrates the difference.

In one of the instances in which Debbie and I were giving a vehicle away, we were standing in our driveway with the couple we were about to bless. There happened to be two vehicles in the driveway at the time—the one we were giving away and ours.

The wife responded to our gift with gratitude. She was very excited and very expressive in her thanks. The husband, on the other hand, was not. As we talked, he kept commenting on how nice *my* car was.

When we stepped into the house a little later, he finally came right out and asked, "Do you think you will ever give that other car away?" I remember thinking, *Not to you!*

We need to be aware that our attitudes toward possessions have a powerful ability to expose the true nature of our hearts. Whether it is greed or gratitude, money and material things will bring it out.

If you are a parent, ask yourself this question: Which attitude am I most motivated to reward in my children—greed or gratitude? Obviously, every good parent wants to reward gratitude—and God is no different.

PEANUT BLESSINGS

When God does a work in our hearts, we give simply to give, not to get. The resulting blessing we receive is the by-product, not the goal.

I saw a beautiful example of this on a trip to Costa Rica to preach at a Bible school. I discovered that every Friday at this Bible school, they have what they call Bless Another Day—a day in which students were encouraged to give to others.

I heard about a student in the school who had no money and worked in the fields of a peanut farmer to pay his tuition. He went to the farmer and said, "I'm wondering if you would withhold from my wages the price of one peanut so that I may have it to give to someone on Bless Another Day?" (Keep in mind how easy it would have been for this young man simply to pocket a peanut or two as he worked in the fields. God can bless people of integrity.) The farmer agreed. So, every Friday, this student would bring one peanut to school and give it to a student in his class.

Not surprisingly, God began to bless this young man who had an unselfish, liberal heart. Before long, he wasn't giving peanuts on Bless Another Day; he was giving money. By the end of the semester, he was also buying pencils and other school supplies for the poorest students.

When we come to the place where we give simply because we have an unselfish, liberal heart of gratitude toward God, we will be well on the road to the blessed life.

By the end of that year, God had blessed him so much that he was able to pay a year's tuition for another student. And by the time he graduated, he was paying the tuition of 10 other students besides himself.

Within a few years of graduating from Bible school, he bought the peanut farm where he used to work and was covering the cost of tuition for scores of students who otherwise would not have been able to afford to go.

And it all started because God did a work in his heart. He gave when all he could give was a peanut. The issue is not the amount we give. The issue is the motive behind our giving.

Does God bless givers? Absolutely! But those promises of blessing are given, not to entice us, but to free us from the fear and grief that keeps so many believers from turning loose and giving.

Yes, when you give, "It will be given to you: good measure, pressed down, shaken together, and running over will be put into your bosom" (Luke 6:38).

God pours blessings on givers, and He does it so they can continue to give even more to His kingdom—but it takes a heart transplant.

When we come to the place where we give simply because we have an unselfish, liberal heart of gratitude toward God, we will be well on the road to the blessed life.

DO THE RIGHT THING

Do you remember that old station wagon of ours I mentioned back in chapter 1? Well, there was a reason we were driving such a "vintage" vehicle. It's not that by the world's way of thinking we couldn't afford anything better. We had purchased an older car because God had instructed us to do three things concerning our finances:

1. Get out of debt.

2. Never manipulate others.

3. Give.

For us, these three very important financial principles have been the foundation stones of living the blessed life. And I think they represent keys to living in God's financial Promised Land for you as well.

So in this chapter, I want to elaborate on these three principles and share some testimonies I believe you'll find both inspiring and instructive.

GET OUT OF DEBT

We purchased that 1973 station wagon with 130,000 miles for a very simple reason. It was the only running vehicle I could find for which we could pay cash. We bought it for $750.

Just prior to that purchase, we had been driving a one-year-old, fully loaded Oldsmobile. It was a big nice car with a big fat payment—$370 per month, to be exact. By way of comparison, our house payment at that time was $320 per month. (Keep in mind, these were early 1980s dollars.) It didn't take long for the Lord to show us how absurd this was from a stewardship standpoint. In fact, it was ridiculous!

God had told us to sell it and work toward getting out of debt, so we did. We then bought that old wagon for $750. We prayed over it. We anointed it with oil (about a quart a week). And we loved it because, though it wasn't much to look at, we knew we were in the center of God's will.

It took us one year to get completely out of debt. I know you may be thinking that it would take you much longer, but let me tell you what we did to make it a reality.

During that season of time, we didn't buy anything that wasn't a true necessity. We didn't go out to eat. We didn't go to the movies. We didn't buy any new clothes. We didn't even buy a new microwave oven when ours broke midway through that year.

We bought nothing during that time because we had made a solemn commitment to get out of debt—no matter how long it took. We said to the Lord, *We are serious about this*, and we showed it.

I've had many people tell me they want to get out of debt, yet they never change their lifestyle. They still eat out all the time. They still spend freely on entertainment and vacations. They still buy new clothes. They even continue to make large purchases on credit, such as new homes and new cars.

I remember one couple in our church who were in serious financial trouble and came to us for counseling. In contrast to most, they actually did what we counseled them to do. (It's amazing to me how many people come to a pastor asking for his or her counsel and then proceed to ignore it after it's given. I don't know why they ask in the first place!)

This couple, however, asked us for counsel, and then they followed through. We told them lovingly but candidly, "You can't afford the house in which you are living. You're going to have to sell it and downsize. You're going to have to take some other radical steps as well."

Amazingly, they actually did it. They followed godly, Spirit-led counsel. The result? God has so blessed that family. As a matter of fact, the couple was recently able to give a car to a young man in our church who needed one.

They went from crushing financial pressure to having the freedom to give a car away. By downsizing, their true standard of living (their levels of joy, peace, and fulfillment) has gone up immeasurably.

The truth is that if you're going to live the lifestyle of a giver, you're going to have to make the lifestyle adjustments that allow you to have something to give. One of the first ways to do that is to get out of debt.

When God saw that we were serious about our commitment to get out of debt, He began to bless us tremendously. That is why we were able to become debt free in only one year.

That's the great thing about this principle. You're never on your own. God stands ready and willing to provide all of heaven's help if only you will take a step of faith and begin.

So let me ask you, How serious are you about obeying God in your finances?

Debbie and I have come to understand that all of our money belongs to Him. Thus, we need to ask Him before we spend any of it. A valuable practice is to pray about every significant financial purchase and wait overnight before you commit.

God stands ready and willing to provide all of heaven's help if only you will take a step of faith and begin.

I'm obviously not talking about praying overnight about whether to go with corn flakes or raisin bran at the grocery store. I am, however, talking about taking almost every purchase—large and small—to the Lord and waiting overnight before making a decision.

You see, I've discovered that about 80 percent of our purchases are made on impulse. A little prayer and a brief cooling-off period can keep us from making countless spending mistakes.

This commitment is especially helpful when you're being pressured by a salesman to make an immediate decision. When a prospect says, "I need to pray about it," many salesmen of big ticket items have been trained to tell you they respect that desire and that they'll leave for a little while and come back in a few minutes. But they don't have an answer when you tell them you don't make any purchases without praying about it overnight.

One of the biggest rewards of obeying God and getting out of debt is the freedom to do the right thing when God speaks to you about it. Let me give you a few examples.

I once had a disgruntled former employee who accused me of cheating him out of $2,500. Now, I had the financial records to show that he was wrong. He was owed no money at all, and I could prove it! But I believe in the principle of going the extra mile, and I know God always blesses me for it.

So we sold a vehicle that we had at the time (we had paid cash, of course, so we owned it outright), bought a less expensive vehicle and took $2,500 of the proceeds and sent it to him.

We didn't owe him the money. But we just felt God saying, "Go the extra mile." The next week, someone sent us a van that cost $25,000.

On another occasion, I had a former employer accuse me of owing him $400. He was wrong. I didn't owe him $400, and I could have proven it. But again, we wanted to go the extra mile. Romans 12 tells us, "If it is possible, as much as depends on you, live peaceably with all men" (v. 18).

Frankly, I would much rather be cheated by men and blessed by God than to insist on fairness from men but forfeit God's blessing. Every time I've done the right thing, God has always blessed me.

So I sent my former employer the $400. The next week, I received an unexpected offering of $5,000. God always honors doing the right thing.

God is looking for good stewards. He's looking for people who "render therefore to Caesar the things that are Caesar's, and to God the things that are God's" (Matthew 22:21). This also means that we shouldn't cheat on our taxes or scrimp on our giving.

Think about it. If God really has done a work in our hearts, why would we be trying to figure out how to diminish the amount of our tithe? Why would we even be trying to rationalize tithing on the net of our income rather than the gross?

That's the key—God wants to do a work in our hearts.

NEVER MANIPULATE OTHERS

The second foundation stone that God laid in our lives came in the form of clear instructions from Him: "Don't manipulate."

When I was a traveling minister, I had a mailing list of people who had donated to my ministry at one time or another. I would periodically send letters to the folks on that list, letting them know what was going on with the ministry and making them aware of the needs we had.

Let me emphasize right now that there is nothing wrong with that. It is appropriate for ministries to maintain a list of donors and to use it to let people know about needs. But I discovered that I had begun to view that mailing list as my source.

For instance, there was a man in Houston, Texas, on that list who faithfully sent us $300 every time he got a letter from us. When the Lord began to deal with me about my heart attitude toward that list, I remember thinking, *But, Lord, if I don't mail to that list, people like that man in Houston might not send the money.* And the Lord responded, "If I want him to give, I'll speak to him."

In obedience, I stopped the mailing list that I had begun to view as my source of provision. And sure enough, the man in Houston stopped sending his $300 donations.

I remember saying to the Lord, "Lord, I thought You said if You wanted him to give, You would speak to him." And the Lord replied by saying, "Well, I'm obviously not speaking to him, am I?"

Thus, the Lord began to show me some things about where I was placing my trust and expectancy for provision. He corrected my focus regarding who my source was.

Obviously, doing the right thing means walking in integrity—no hidden agendas and no hidden motives. Again, there is nothing unethical about a ministry maintaining a mailing list. What is wrong is starting to view the people on that list as your source rather than God. When you fall into that trap, it becomes very easy to move over into manipulation in order to get people to give.

In my case, I had slowly stopped looking to God to meet our needs and had begun to look to people instead.

If you're in vocational ministry as a pastor, missionary, or evangelist, or in some other type of ministry in which your support comes from offerings and donations, this is an area in which you must always be on your guard. But this is really a trap anyone can fall into.

Who are *you* viewing as your source? To whom are you looking for provision? Do you ever drop hints when you're around people who are in a position to help you?

I'll elaborate in the next chapter, but I'll tell you right now that people who operate in the gift of giving have the ability to discern manipulation in others quite quickly. And the Lord will not allow them to reward manipulation.

To be blunt, manipulation is a form of witchcraft. It's relying on our ability to speak and persuade rather than on God's ability to speak and persuade. God can get provision to you without your manipulative help!

For example, in an elders' meeting at the church I pastor, we all felt a leading to send a financial gift to a particular church for their building fund. This is not a church with which we have a close relationship. In fact, we had never even met with their leadership. All we knew was the Holy Spirit was speaking to us about helping them. They were probably praying for provision, and God found some willing ears in our elders.

God is able to meet all of our needs, but He will not do so if we are relying on manipulation. As with everything else we've discussed in this book thus far, it's all a matter of the heart.

I go out of my way to avoid even the appearance of manipulation. For example, in almost 20 years of teaching and preaching on giving, I have never once received an offering for our ministry after I have taught on giving. Instead, I've always encouraged the listeners to give first to their local churches and to the material needs in the church body and to other ministries.

I will not have a traveling minister in my pulpit who is willing to receive offerings for himself after he preaches on giving. Sadly, there are plenty who not only are willing but also insist on it.

I have a pastor friend whose church was struggling financially. On someone else's recommendation, he called a well-known minister who is known for preaching about money. He was simply seeking some counsel and some ideas for communicating truths to his people about giving.

This minister told him that he wanted to come and help him personally. He offered to come preach for him on the subject of giving. My pastor friend accepted this offer.

This minister came and taught the people the concept of paying back tithes (the idea is that if you have gotten behind on tithing, you need to catch up). I personally don't see that concept taught anywhere in Scripture. On the contrary, as with any other area of our lives in which we fall short, the answer is repentance, not restitution. Jesus has paid the price in full for *all* of our sins, and we can never repay Him.

Nevertheless, the people responded to that minister's message and gave more than $60,000 in the offering. Following the service, this minister told the pastor that the entire offering should go to him, not the church. "You'll be blessed by sowing this offering into my ministry," the pastor was told.

That was pure manipulation. That preacher left that church no better off than he found it. I'm convinced those kinds of things are an abomination to the Lord.

At the risk of sounding as if I'm boasting (Believe me, I'm not. This is all due to the grace of God.), I must tell you that in every church in which I've ever preached on giving, the pastor has always told me later how much healthier the church was afterward.

If you want your heart to follow after the things that God's heart is after—the local church and reaching the lost—put your treasure there.

Several churches have seen their resources double, and some have even tripled, once the people caught a revelation of the joy of tithing and giving. And it isn't just the finances that increase in these cases. Peace and joy in the church increase. Attendance increases. And the numbers of people serving and volunteering increase. The intensity of their worship increases. All of these are vital signs of church health. They all happen when people allow God to do a work in their hearts through giving.

Why is this so? I think the answer lies in Matthew 6:21. Remember that in this verse, Jesus said, "For where your treasure is, there your heart will be also." When people begin to invest their treasure in God through the local church, their hearts follow.

It's the same dynamic you see when someone invests in the stock market for the first time. When you invest in a stock, you start keeping up with it. You begin checking on it in the newspaper or on the Internet every few days. You start listening for news about that company on television. Why? Because wherever your treasure is, your heart's going to go there also.

If you want your heart to follow after the things that God's heart is after—the local church and reaching the lost—put your treasure there. Your heart will follow.

When God's people catch a revelation of giving—when God does a work in their hearts—they begin to want to serve in their churches. They want to help the children's ministry grow. They want the church to have a good youth ministry, a powerful choir, and a blessed staff. They want to be generous in missionary giving.

The whole atmosphere in a church changes when people catch the revelation of generosity, tithing, and giving.

GIVE!

Yes, God has said, "Get out of debt." He has said, "Never manipulate people." And the third thing God instructed us to do in the area of our finances was "Give." We are to begin giving generously—not just tithing, but giving well above our tithes.

I remember the first time Debbie and I began to give over and above our tithe on a regular basis. God immediately began to bless and multiply our income. After some prayer, we had committed to give 10 percent of our gross income as our tithe to our local church and an additional 10 percent of gross income to missions. That year, as we doubled our giving, God doubled our income.

Thus far, I've shared many testimonies with you about our own giving. Now let me relate a few amazing testimonies that have developed as I have preached this message to others.

There was a family in a church at which I was scheduled to preach that had borrowed $1,200 from another family in the church during a personal crisis in their lives. The other family didn't need the money back and had even told them not to worry about repaying it.

But the family that had borrowed the money felt strongly that, in order to be good stewards, they needed to pay it back quickly. That became a focus of their prayer. They asked God for the ability to repay the loan.

On a certain night, I was preparing to preach on the subject of giving. That very afternoon, the family that had borrowed the money was watching Pat Robertson's *700 Club*. As they watched, Dr. Robertson shared a prophetic word about a family who owed a debt. He said God was about to provide a way for them to pay it back supernaturally. With excitement, they took hold of that word in faith.

That evening, I preached, as planned, on giving. I encouraged the people to give first to their church and then to wherever else the Holy Spirit prompted them to give. As I did, people began to spontaneously go to that family and put money in their pockets. When they got home, they pulled it out and put it on the kitchen table. They counted exactly $1,200. The next night, they were joyously able to pay the family back every cent they had borrowed.

On another occasion, I was preaching on giving in a church in which one of the members had been severely injured in a car wreck and was temporarily in a wheelchair. Because of his injuries, the doctors had told him he would be in the wheelchair for about three months and then on crutches for another three months.

At the time when I preached there, it had only been about two weeks since the accident. The old truck he had been driving in the accident had been completely destroyed and was uninsured.

The night that I preached, many people went to him and gave him money at the prompting of the Lord. When he got home, he counted $2,000—the exact amount of an old pickup he had found to replace the one that had been totaled.

As he prayed about it, however, the Lord showed him 20 people to whom he was supposed to give $100 each. God had done a work in his heart where giving was concerned too.

The next night, he went to each person and gave him or her the money, just as the Lord had instructed him. A few days later, the Lord spoke to another man in the church to buy him a brand-new pickup truck. The man was to take it over to the injured man and to pray for him to be healed.

> ## God wants to work miracles in our lives, and many times He starts by working miracles in our hearts regarding financial obedience.

The man prayed for him, and God miraculously healed him on the spot. The next morning, he drove his new truck to work!

Giving touches at the core of so much of what God wants to do in our lives. God wants to work miracles in our lives, and many times He starts by working miracles in our hearts regarding financial obedience.

TRUST AND OBEY

Once I was teaching the principles of giving in a church, and we were seeing a tremendous move of God's Spirit among the people. People were responding and giving to the church and to one another as the Lord led them.

One night, a couple who were seemingly broken before the Lord came up to me. They were weeping almost uncontrollably. They said that the Lord had spoken to them about giving away every penny they had. I learned that they had written a check for all the money they had in the world. Now they were bringing me the check, saying, "We're supposed to give this to you. Do whatever you feel you're supposed to do with it."

Immediately, I knew what the Lord wanted me to do. When they handed me the check, I asked them, "Are you saying this is mine now, and I can do anything that I want with it?" Through their tears, they nodded and answered yes. So, I said, "Well, I know exactly what the Lord would have me do with this check." Then I tore it up in front of them. Immediately, they fell to the floor and began to weep uncontrollably.

God did a wondrous work in their hearts that night—one that changed them for the rest of their lives. They were never the same. They had passed a major test of obedience.

To this day, I don't know how much money it was, nor do I care. I do know it was enormous in their eyes and precious in the eyes of God. I also know that no amount of money in the world could purchase what God did in that couple's lives that night.

That incident reminds me of a spiritual principle that my wife and I have come to call the IO Principle. IO stands for Instant Obedience. We have come to understand the importance of responding instantly when we hear God's voice.

With that couple, I could have waited to see how much the check was for. I could have pocketed it, prayed about it further, and torn it up later. But that would have been dangerous.

Sometimes in giving, if you wait, Satan is given time to come up with all kinds of good reasons *not* to do what God has told you to do. The longer you wait, the more time there is for your mind and emotions to cloud the message.

If God speaks, do it. Trust and obey. And do it now! Don't give Satan an opportunity to help you rationalize another course of action. Follow the I. O. Principle.

And remember that the three elements I have outlined here: (1) getting out of debt, (2) avoiding manipulation of others, and (3) giving as God leads you to give, represent the foundation of the blessed life. I'm convinced of it.

Lay that foundation and watch miracles begin to happen in your finances.

THE GIFT
OF GIVING

Many people are surprised to discover that there is a spiritual gift of giving that is every bit as valid as the gifts of prophecy and teaching.

We tend to hear and read a lot about various spiritual gifts. But for some reason, we hear very little about the gift of giving. But the fact is, it is mentioned prominently in Romans 12:

> Having then gifts differing according to the grace that is given to
> us, let us use them: if prophecy, let us prophesy in proportion to our
> faith; or ministry, let us use it in our ministering; he who teaches, in
> teaching; he who exhorts, in exhortation; *he who gives, with liberality*;
> he who leads, with diligence; he who shows mercy, with cheerfulness
> (vv. 6–8, emphasis added).

This passage outlines seven motivational gifts. They are often called motivational gifts because they tend to identify what most motivates the one who has the gift. I believe every Christian has one of these as his or her primary gifting. Of course, a fully functioning Spirit-filled Christian should have all of these gifts in operation to various degrees. Jesus walked in all of the gifts in full measure.

We, on the other hand, might have two or three of these gifts that are very prevalent in our lives, but one in particular will be the main motivating gift for us. That's why it takes all of us working together to comprise the body of Christ.

In the verses we just read, we found prophecy, ministry (or serving), teaching, exhortation, giving, leading (or administration), and mercy. These are the seven motivational gifts of the Spirit. Here's a quick definition of each of these:

- Prophecy—reveals the motives of man and seeks conformity to God's Word and ways.

- Ministry (or serving)—meets needs on a practical basis.

- Teaching—searches out and presents scriptural truths.

- Exhortation—admonishes or encourages others.

- Giving—meets material needs, often through finances.

- Leading (or administration)—organizes and leads.

- Mercy—empathizes and shows compassion to others.

Many people are also unaware of the verses that immediately follow the ones we just read. Romans 12:9-15 provides information that correlates with each gift.

For example, verse 9 speaks to those with the gift of prophecy: "Let love be without hypocrisy. Abhor what is evil. Cling to what is good." That is what someone with the motivation of prophecy does; they abhor things that are evil, and they cling to what is good. But the admonition to them from Scripture is to "let love be without hypocrisy." In other words, love everyone—the good and the bad.

Verse 10 provides encouragement for those with the gift of serving: "Be kindly affectionate to one another with brotherly love, in honor giving preference to one another." That's a great description of someone who serves with excellence.

Verse 11 correlates with the gift of teaching: "Not lagging in diligence, fervent in spirit, serving the Lord." Teachers tend to be very diligent, but their admonition from Scripture is to be fervent when they teach the truths that the Lord has given them from Scripture.

The next verse, verse 12, offers instruction for those with the gift of exhortation: "Rejoicing in hope, patient in tribulation, continuing steadfastly in prayer." People who are exhorters know how to rejoice, but they also know how to be patient with people. They are also wonderful intercessors—praying for people in need.

And in verse 13, we find the job description of someone with the gift of giving: "Distributing to the needs of the saints, given to hospitality." The people I know who function in the gift of giving truly love to distribute to the needs of the saints. They are also very hospitable, always opening up their homes to others. Some givers I know have actually built extra rooms onto their homes so that missionaries can stay with them when they come in from the field.

Verse 14 correlates with leading or administrating. It says, "Bless those who persecute you; bless and do not curse." This is certainly something that those in places of authority must do all the time. People who lead are no strangers to having people speak against them.

Finally, verse 15 correlates with the gift of mercy: "Rejoice with those who rejoice, and weep with those who weep." You don't really have to tell people who have the gift of mercy to weep with those who weep; it comes naturally. But you do sometimes have to admonish them to rejoice with those who rejoice.

THINGS TO LOOK OUT FOR

As you know by now, my wife and I, by God's grace, have been used in the area of giving for many years. I have shared about a remarkable season of time in which we were able to give nine vehicles away in 18 months. Since that time, we've been able to give away several more. Blessing people is fun (and habit forming!).

Since those early days, we've been able to give our first house away. We've gone through seasons in our lives in which we've given 70 percent of our income away. And on three different occasions in our lives, we've had the privilege of giving everything that we own away. (I'll share some details about the most recent of these times in the closing chapter of this book.)

Please understand, I'm not telling you any of this to brag. I'm not interested in patting myself on the back. I am interested, however, in letting you know that I have *lived* the principles I'm sharing with you. This isn't theory with me—it's real life.

Because we've been able to walk in the area of giving for many years, we've learned some things. We've learned a lot about those who operate in the gift of giving, and we've learned a lot about how people respond to those who have the gift of giving.

I remember, for instance, a time the Lord spoke to us about giving $1,000 to some acquaintances who had a need. When we gave them the money, their response to us was, "Of course, $1,000 to you guys is like only $100 to a lot of people." The implication was that we had more money than we knew what to do with and that giving $1,000 away was not a sacrifice for us.

This hurt us, and we didn't understand why they would make such a statement. We had just given them $1,000. Why wasn't their response, "Thank you so much!"? Why would they say, "Of course, $1,000 to you guys is like only $100 to a lot of people"?

That wasn't true, of course. A thousand dollars has the same purchasing power regardless of who is holding it. Yet often that's exactly the way we think about people the Lord has blessed financially. Statements like the one that couple made reveal insensitivity, ingratitude, and wrong thinking about money.

It reminds me of another couple who was aware of our reputation as generous givers. Every time we were around them, they would start dropping hints about all their financial needs. When it seemed to them that we weren't picking up their "subtle" hints, they got increasingly blatant. Of course, we were picking up their hints; we just had no intention of responding to manipulation.

I remember one occasion when one of them said, "Yeah, we were short this month on some of our bills, but of course, you two wouldn't know anything about that." Of course, we knew quite well what it's like to have too much month at the end of our money. We had experienced times in which we had to trust God for the meeting of our basic needs. Even people who have been blessed tremendously by God still know times in which they've had shortfalls.

The unfortunate truth is that if you operate in the spiritual gift of giving, you are almost certainly going to encounter the ungrateful, the insensitive, or the manipulative. It comes with the territory.

A WORD TO PASTORS

This chapter holds some valuable insights for pastors. I really have a heart to help shepherds understand that people in their churches have this gift, how to recognize it, and how to cultivate it.

It's kind of odd. Many pastors instinctively know that they need to nurture, train, and develop people in the church who have the gifts of leading, serving, or teaching. They will instruct them and help them learn to function better in their gifts. But many of the same pastors don't even know *how* to recognize the gift of giving as a spiritual gift, and if they do, they don't know how to help people grow in it. I suspect some pastors even think it is somehow inappropriate for them to develop those members who have the gift of giving.

Think about this. Since there are seven motivational gifts, it's quite possible that one out of seven of those sitting around you in church has the motivational gift of giving. If you are one of those with the gift of giving, I want to help you. And I want to help the leaders who are reading this book to know better how to help people with this gift. They are too valuable to the body of Christ not to have their gifts matured and developed.

If you have the motivational gift of giving, I want you to know it is a wonderful spiritual gift from God. You should be pleased and grateful that God has given you this gift. My hope is that you will see it as a spiritual gift that God wants to use to build the Church and to build His kingdom.

If you're a pastor or a leader, I want to challenge you to ask God to take you to a higher level of giving in your own life. It's very difficult for a pastor to lead givers effectively if that pastor doesn't have a heart for giving or an understanding of the biblical principles of stewardship.

I encourage pastors to preach on giving without apology. Money was the subject in 30 percent of the parables Jesus taught. I like to preach on giving because I know it helps people. I know that when people hear and embrace the truth about Spirit-led giving, God is going to bless them and change their lives for the better.

In all truth and sincerity, when I preach to my congregation about giving, my motive is to help *them*, not the church. I will say, however, that I personally don't care for some of the phrases that are commonly used related to giving in church.

Money was the subject in 30 percent of the parables Jesus taught.

For instance, a vocational minister will often stand before the congregation and say, "*I'm* going to *receive* the offering now." It suggests that the congregants are the givers and the pastor and staff are the receivers. I would very much prefer to hear, "*We're* all going to *give* our offerings now." This indicates that the pastor is joining the people in giving to the Lord.

Oh, how I long to see pastors ask God to do a work in their hearts in the area of giving—then preach with passion and power out of that changed heart. Some don't because they are afraid people will be offended. I have heard them say so. But the truth is that the only people who get offended when you preach on giving are the ones who don't give—those who are in the grasp of the spirit of mammon. The people who have a revelation of giving will not get offended when you preach on it, and those in bondage to mammon can never taste freedom unless they hear the truth.

People who have the gift of giving are a wonderful asset to a church. A pastor can go to a genuine giver and directly share a need with them, and they will not be offended. As a matter of fact, they will appreciate it because of their strong desire to meet needs.

I had one man with the gift of giving describe how givers will frequently direct the majority of their above-the-tithe offerings toward ministries outside the church. Why? Because the church's vision simply isn't big enough to justify the funds they would like to give. In other words, the pastors either don't have a big enough vision or big enough faith to be able to attract those funds.

I want to say to pastors, "Get a large vision from God, because He has given the gift of giving to individuals in your church who have a desire to give large amounts if the vision is large and worthy."

Of course, as I have already stated, if you begin looking to them as your source, rather than God, you won't see much in the way of results. People with the gift of giving can sense manipulation from a mile away. If you start dropping hints around them instead of making a straightforward request, they will be offended and will not give. People who have the gift of giving can pick up on gimmicks and scams quicker than anyone else because they give by supernatural revelation. They give by the voice of the Spirit.

I remember one particular lunch meeting I had with a fairly new acquaintance. He was wealthy, and I could discern that he had the gift of giving—though at the time it was clearly undeveloped.

Soon after we sat down, he said, "Let's get something straight right from the start. I will only give to your ministry if God tells me to." A little startled at his bluntness, I said, "Great! I'd like to get something straight right from the start as well. Like you, I function in the gift of giving and I didn't invite you to lunch to ask you for money. Frankly, God has blessed us tremendously, and we don't need any of your money. I'm here because God has given me some insights about the gift of giving. The Lord told me that you don't know these principles, even though you have this gift."

At this point, he was the one who was startled. Now on a roll, I continued, "The Lord showed me that there are five things you have been praying about doing. I can help you apply your gift of giving in these areas if you'll let me."

I outlined the five issues the Lord had shown me, and in addition to being amazed at the accuracy, he admitted that he did indeed need help in those areas.

Since that occasion, we have become close friends. Today, he has surpassed me in his understanding in this area and frequently helps me teach others about the gift of giving.

THE SIN OF PARTIALITY

The Bible strongly discourages us from showing partiality, specifically toward the wealthy or prominent in society. "But if you show partiality, you commit sin, and are convicted by the law as transgressors" (James 2:9).

I have observed that when it comes to relating to people who have the gift of giving, we frequently show partiality and that it manifests itself in two distinct ways.

To be sure, there are occasions in which a church goes out of its way to treat a wealthy visitor better than it should. But my personal observation has been that the rich are often treated much worse than others, usually because of envy, jealousy, or greed.

In my experience, people who have exercised the gift of giving faithfully—and have been blessed with finances as a result—don't really want to be treated any differently from anyone else. But often, people who have great financial resources are some of the loneliest people in the world.

By and large, people of wealth have been badly treated by the church. They have sat in services as jokes were made about "the rich." They've heard sermon illustrations from the pulpit that have portrayed success as if it were a sin or something about which to be ashamed. Then some pastors wonder why people of influence and money don't come to their churches. In having this attitude, many pastors and Christians have been infected by the world's way of thinking.

Resentment of success and excellence is a hallmark of the world's system today. Think for a moment about any of the Hollywood movies or television programs you have seen lately. In how many of them was the "bad guy" a successful businessperson? The "evil rich person" and the "greedy corporation" have become Hollywood clichés.

Watch enough Hollywood entertainment, and you will soon find yourself thinking that everyone who does well in life must have lied, cheated, and backstabbed to achieve it. This lie resonates with people because it appeals to envy and jealousy in the fallen human nature.

In reality, people who do well over the long haul tend to be people who do things God's way (whether they know it or not!).

Consider the following Scriptures:

> The Lord makes poor and makes rich; He brings low and lifts up. He raises the poor from the dust and lifts the beggar from the ash heap (1 Samuel 2:7-8).

> He who has a slack hand becomes poor, but the hand of the diligent makes rich (Proverbs 10:4).

> The blessing of the Lord makes one rich, and He adds no sorrow with it (Proverbs 10:22).

> The generous soul will be made rich, and he who waters will also be watered himself (Proverbs 11:25).

According to these Scriptures, wealth is a blessing from God and a product of things such as diligence and generosity.

So let me ask you, Why would we put down someone whom God has blessed? Why would we consider something that came from the hand of God to be evil or shameful? It borders on blasphemy.

I suggest we need to change our attitudes about money. We need to examine our hearts and see if we have any prejudices against people who have been blessed financially. Envy and jealousy are rampant in our culture and, sadly, in our churches. It is possible to have your thinking tainted by the spirit of this age.

Abram might not have been welcome in many churches today. Why? "Abram was very rich in livestock, in silver, and in gold" (Genesis 13:2).

Many of the men in the Bible whom we revere and respect as men of faith were blessed financially by God. They were blessed because they were good stewards, and God knew that He could trust them with wealth. He knew they would use their resources to bless others and carry out God's purposes.

We need to examine our hearts, including our feelings toward those who seem to live extravagantly by our standards. For example, let me tell you about a friend of mine who is very well-to-do.

My friend made the foundation of his house with precious stones. His driveway is made of gold and his gates are made of pearls. Do you know who I'm talking about? I'm talking about God. Would you say that He is eccentric? Would you say that He has a problem in this area?

The problem, of course, is not money. The problem is how we think about money and those who have more of it than we do.

Like the rest of us, people with wealth are just looking for a place where they can be accepted. Unfortunately, I think we have treated them so badly in the church that much of their giving now goes to parachurch ministries and Christian charities rather than to a local church.

Please understand, I'm not opposed to people with the gift of giving donating to ministries other than a local church, but I would also like to see local churches get all the resources God wants them to have.

I have a passion to see churches financially able to hire the staff, build the buildings, and send the missionaries they need to fulfill God's highest calling. That can only happen as churches quit ignoring (or even despising) one of the seven gifts the Spirit provides in the body.

HALLMARKS OF A GIVER

Of course, for every truth of God, Satan tries to offer a distorted counterfeit.

For example, I believe God tried to restore the truth about giving to the church in the 1980s. But Satan distorted that truth; thus, we saw many ministers exploit people and gather large sums of money for their own pleasure. The abuses were there for the whole world to see. Yes, God wants to bless His people, but for the right purposes.

As we've seen, the gift of giving is one of seven motivational gifts. If those gifts are evenly distributed among God's people then roughly 15 percent of believers have this gift. Yet surveys show that only 5 to 7 percent of Christians believe they have the gift of giving.

Why is this? Is it because we haven't recognized it as a valid gift from our pulpits? Is this because we don't honor people who have this gift, equipping them and encouraging them in it?

For every truth of God, Satan tries to offer a distorted counterfeit.

Let me describe the classic signs of a believer with the gift of giving and the way you can recognize them in your own heart and in others. I also want to help pastors recognize this gift in their people and be better able to equip them to operate in that gift, to the building up of the Church.

- *People who have the gift of giving respond to strong vision with clear objectives.* They want their money to count; they want to see ministries and ministers that operate by sound financial principles; they want to invest in ministries and ministers that are good stewards and are successful in using the funds God is giving them. They are literally *investors* in the kingdom. And as good investors, they want to put their money in good ministries that are being effective with the funds entrusted to them. This is very important to them.

- *Givers can be men or women.* I know a man in our church who is very successful financially, but his wife is the one who has the motivational gift of giving. Now, he loves to give too but she is the one who hears the Lord by revelation in the area of giving. His motivational gift is that of leadership, which God uses to produce financial blessing. Then she is able to use her gift of giving to distribute those finances as the Lord speaks to both of them. Now, obviously, they each have other gifts as well, but these are strong motivational gifts with them. They make a great team.

- *People who have the gift of giving have discernment that allows them to determine genuine needs.* Remember, we're talking about a spiritual gift that comes from God. Therefore, a person who has this gift picks up manipulation more quickly than anyone can by natural means. They are able to look at ministries and missionaries and determine where bona fide needs are and how money should be used. People who have the gift of giving are great at serving on mission committees and benevolence committees, because they have the ability to determine true needs that are worthy of investment by the church.

- *People who have the gift of giving are very frugal but also very generous.* Let me explain. A while back, I had to counsel lovingly a man with the gift of giving who was out of balance in this way. He would joyously give away thousands of dollars as the Lord prompted but then turn around and pore over his wife's grocery receipts to see if she had spent a few dollars needlessly. He wasn't trying to be mean; he was just letting the frugality that comes naturally to a giver get way out of balance. Because he didn't understand some things in the area of giving, he didn't realize he was being generous toward strangers but stingy toward the most important person in his life. Nevertheless, people who have this gift tend to watch where their money goes. They like budgets, and they understand the principles of finance very well. Their greatest joy comes in meeting needs.

- *A person who has the gift of giving desires to be appreciated but not recognized.* They don't want their name on anything; they don't want to be praised in front of their church for their giving; they don't want any recognition for their gift; but they do like to know that their obedience and sacrifices are appreciated. A heartfelt thank-you goes a long, long way.

- *People who have the gift of giving want to invest in a stable ship, not a sinking ship.* When a television minister says, "If you don't give, we're going off the air," people who have the gift of giving will tend to disqualify that ministry. When, on the other hand, a television ministry credibly shows that it is actually helping people, feeding people, taking care of people, and getting people saved—those who have the gift of giving will favor that ministry. A person who has the gift of giving doesn't want to invest in a sinking ship or even one that is drifting aimlessly with the current. They want their money to be handled in a prudent manner, and they appreciate excellence and quality. One faithful giver told me that if the head of a ministry or organization has a poverty mentality or the wrong perspective about money, he doesn't want to invest in that ministry. He chooses to invest in ministries where the leader has demonstrated the ability to handle large sums of money in a prudent and wise way.

- *Contrary to common belief, people who truly have the gift of giving don't want to control their money after they have given it.* If you encounter a person who attempts to assert control through the giving of their money, you can be sure they are not operating in the spiritual gift of giving. People who have the gift of giving want to give generously, and as I have stated, they need to know that their money will be handled correctly. But they never ever want to try to control or manipulate with their money. Most of the time, they will give to ministries that have strong leaders with a strong vision. (Just a note to pastors here: You obviously need to respect and appreciate people who have this gift. But you can't minister to anyone with whom you are overly impressed or who intimidates you. As I've said, givers with wealth want to be treated like everyone else.)

- *People who have the gift of giving don't want to be a band-aid—they want to be a cure.* In other words, they don't want their money just to provide a short-term fix of something that is going to break again. They want it to bring lasting solutions to situations.

- *People who have the gift of giving want to give more than money—they want to give their time, their talent, and their wisdom.* Many givers are quite talented. Judson Cornwall calls them "Apostles in the business world."[1] In our church, there is a man with the gift of giving who has saved us thousands of dollars on our land and building acquisitions. He has tremendous wisdom and discernment in this area, and his counsel is very valuable; but he also has tremendous wisdom in many other areas. For example, he is a very gifted Bible teacher and leader, in the church and on the mission field. In fact, a few years ago he helped a new church in Odessa, Ukraine, pattern their church government after ours. I've discovered that people who have the gift of giving love to see their experience and expertise put to work for the kingdom. They want to offer wise counsel to the church they love and appreciate. By the same token, if you reject their wisdom, counsel, and experience, they will most likely find a ministry that wants it.

- *People who have the gift of giving are often gifted leaders.* Their ability to lead is frequently the reason they have been so successful.

- *As I have already stated, people who have the gift of giving don't appreciate being put down or criticized for having a successful lifestyle.* (Who *does* enjoy being resented or criticized unjustly?) If wealthy believers have large homes, they most likely see them as investments that are actually building wealth that they will ultimately be able to use in the kingdom of God. The income that God has blessed them with may give them the ability to drive nice vehicles and have nice clothes. For them, it's not about extravagance or being ostentatious; it's about enjoying some of the fruits of God's blessing. Nevertheless, on many occasions, I have heard pastors deride, criticize, and generalize about people who have nice possessions, apparently unaware that they are ridiculing people whom God has blessed with the gift of giving. Often, the people being criticized are giving away a much higher percentage of their incomes than that preacher would ever dream of doing himself.

- *Successful people with the gift of giving don't want to talk about money all the time.* I know many pastors who always want to talk about money when they get around people who have the gift of giving. I've discovered that's not the subject they want to discuss. Money to them is a tool—not something to be worshipped, obsessed over, or analyzed all the time. Ask about their family. Find out what their kids are doing. Talk about what you've both been seeing in the Word lately. When you're around someone with the gift of giving, talk about anything but money.

ADVICE FOR GIVERS

It is very possible that, as you've read this book, you have been stirred because you

Invest your money where it will make the largest possible impact for the kingdom of God.

recognized in yourself the hallmarks of someone to whom God has given the gift of giving.

If so, I would encourage you to learn more about that important gift. Do your own Bible study on the subject. And if you are not already tithing, begin to tithe at your local church and look for places where your money can be best invested in the kingdom. Look for opportunities to bless worthy ministries that are affecting and helping people.

Begin "distributing to the needs of the saints," as you are "given to hospitality" (Romans 12:13). Invest your money where it will make the largest possible impact for the kingdom of God.

If you have been mistreated or maligned by uninformed people in the church, forgive them. Don't let it cause you to get bitter in your heart and stop the flow of giving and blessing in your life.

Remember, God has caused you to be a river, not a reservoir. The water in a river is pure and clean, but the water in a reservoir is contaminated. Make sure that you are continuing to give, as God leads you, to the church and to worthy ministries that are making an impact for the kingdom of God.

09

GOD REWARDS
GOOD STEWARDSHIP

F or most of us, summer camp holds a lot of interesting memories. For instance, I remember coming to the end of my first week of camp and hearing that there was going to be an awards ceremony. I remember thinking, *An awards ceremony? Not fair! They should have told us at the first of the week that they were going to give out awards. If I had known, I would have tried harder!*

I don't want you to suffer a similar fate. Right now, while you have the rest of your life in front of you, I want to let you know that God is a rewarder.

Hebrews 11 says so in clear terms:

> But without faith it is impossible to please Him, for he who comes to God must believe that He is, *and that He is a rewarder of those who diligently seek Him* (v. 6, emphasis added).

God is a rewarder. This is a truth about God of which many Christians don't seem to be aware. He loves to reward us when we diligently seek His presence, His will, and His ways. He rewards good work, and He rewards good stewardship.

I had some real-life experiences with this principle when my oldest son was away at college. He had always been a hard-working kid, but he took an accelerated degree program that was so concentrated, it made working a part-time job unfeasible. That meant that I provided nearly all of his support.

Right before he first went off to school, we sat down and drew up a budget for him based upon a set amount I would send him each month.

Two or three months later, we sat down and looked at his budget to see how he was doing. I was pleased to discover that he was doing a great job of living within his means. He wasn't going out to eat or to see movies a lot. He wasn't breaking his budget with new clothes. Essentially, he was being a good steward of the money I was sending him.

God loves to reward us when we diligently seek His presence, His will, and His ways.

So what did a loving father do for his good-steward son? I rewarded him! I increased the amount of money I was sending him each month. I said, "Now, do anything you want with the extra money—go out to eat with your friends after church a few more times or buy a new shirt or two."

A few months later, he called me and said, "Dad, I've been thinking. If I move into a different apartment, I can lower my living expenses and save you some money." Of course, I was blessed to see that he was thinking of ways to help. He knew that his mother and I were sacrificing and economizing on our end to make college possible for him. He had a thankful heart.

We checked into his idea, worked out all the details, and helped him move into the less expensive apartment. Shortly thereafter, he called and said, "It's working out like we thought; you can lower the amount you're sending me now."

Do you know what I did? I kept sending the same amount to him. I said, "Thanks, Son, but now you'll just have more spending money. You've been a good steward, and I want you to be rewarded. You should enjoy the benefits of your good stewardship."

Why don't we expect God to be at least as gracious and responsive as I was to my own son? Why would we be surprised to learn that God rewards and blesses us for being good stewards?

According to Matthew 6, God rewards us when we pray or fast or give to the poor. And in 1 Corinthians, we find:

> Now he who plants and he who waters are one, and *each one will receive his own reward* according to his own labor (3:8, emphasis added).

In Bruce Wilkinson's wonderful book *A Life God Rewards*, he cites example after example of how God is going to reward us in heaven for all the good works that we have done on earth. As he is careful to point out, we're not saved *by* good works, but we are saved *for* good works—and those good works result in rewards.

The familiar words of Ephesians 2 tell us:

> For by grace you have been saved through faith, and that not of yourselves; it is the gift of God, not of works, lest anyone should boast. For we are His workmanship, *created in Christ Jesus for good works*, which God prepared beforehand that we should walk in them (vv. 8–10, emphasis added).

As Bruce points out in his book, we must distinguish between belief and behavior. Our belief determines *where* we will spend eternity, and our behavior determines *how* we will spend eternity.

Bruce is right. God *is* going to reward us one day for our behavior or our good works. But it is also true that God rewards us while we're still here on earth! The Bible makes this quite clear. Look, for example, at Mark 10:

> So Jesus answered and said, "Assuredly, I say to you, there is no one who has left house or brothers or sisters or father or mother or wife or children or lands, for My sake and the gospel's, who shall not receive a hundredfold now *in this time*—houses and brothers and sisters and mothers and children and lands, with persecutions—and *in the age to come*, eternal life" (vv. 29–30, emphasis added).

Jesus is speaking here. What He's saying is "God is going to reward us, not only in the age to come, but *now* in this time as well."

> ## Our belief determines *where we will spend eternity, and our behavior determines* how *we will spend eternity.*

As several of Jesus' parables illustrate, the Lord rewards stewardship. For example, in Luke 19, Jesus relates the parable of the minas. (A "mina" was a coin with a value of about 50 shekels of silver.) Jesus tells of 10 people who received one mina each from a master or lord who wanted to test their stewardship, faithfulness, and ability. As Jesus tells it, when the master returned for an accounting, he instantly rewarded the steward who had done well:

> And he said to him, "Well done, good servant; because you were faithful in a very little, have authority over ten cities" (Luke 19:17).

God is not going to give us more money if we can't even be faithful with the money that He has already given us. If a person can't handle $500 per week, why would God give him $5,000 per week?

God is interested in building His kingdom. That's why He is going to entrust funds to people who are proving to Him that they will be good stewards with those funds—giving when God tells them to give. They won't squander their resources on useless things; they'll budget their money and be accountable. They will also be good stewards of their time, relationships, and talents. This is the message in the parable of the minas. Jesus makes a similar point in the parable of the talents (see Matthew 25:14-30). God gives talents to each of us according to our ability, and He expects us to use those talents for Him and for His kingdom purposes. We will never see God's miraculous power given to poor stewards!

In the parable of the minas, Jesus said to each man who had received a mina, "Do business till I come" (Luke 19:13). That is what God expects us to do. He expects us to do business—kingdom business—until He returns.

In Acts 2, we find the first Spirit-filled Christians so in love with God that they actually sold their possessions and goods—distributing freely to everyone who had need! In response to their generosity and selflessness, God was generous with miracles! They abandoned themselves to God's plan and purpose, and God applauded from heaven by pouring out His power.

In Jesus' parable of the minas, why did the master take the one mina from the bad steward and give it to the one who had 10? Because Jesus is into rewarding stewardship! Poor stewards lose resources; good stewards receive more. It's a pretty simple concept!

Have you ever lamented the fact that it seems that the rich keep getting richer and the poor keep getting poorer? We'd better get used to it. As the parables show, a version of that happens in the kingdom of God. The Lord gives more to those who demonstrate trustworthiness, as my son demonstrated to me when he went away to college. Conversely, God is not going to give more to someone who is irresponsible with money or who doesn't know where his money is going.

Some believers think they are exempt from having to think about stewardship because they don't make very much. They fail to comprehend that it is being faithful with the little that leads to being entrusted with more.

Whenever there is a news report about someone winning the lottery or inheriting a large sum of money, I hear people make statements like this: "Boy, if I inherited 5 million dollars, I'd give a million of it to my church. Yessiree!" Right! What makes them think they will give 20 percent of a windfall to the Lord if they are not even giving 10 percent of their income now? It's because they think, *I will still have plenty left over for myself.* But the heart of stewardship says, "With what I have now,

I'm going to honor God. I will find a way to give 20 percent (or whatever the Spirit directs) now." It is the person with such a heart who is entrusted with more.

Look again at the parable of the talents in Matthew 25. It says the man "called his own servants and delivered his goods to them" (v. 14).

We're like those servants. God has delivered His goods to us. Not only does He entrust us with a measure of material wealth, but He gives us much more precious things as well. He has delivered treasures to us: prayer, the good news of salvation, and the power to help people. These are His precious goods He has delivered to us, and He expects us to use and distribute them.

God expects us to be good stewards of His people whom He puts in our path. And as we've seen, He is a rewarder of good stewards.

You'll remember that Jesus told us in Matthew 6 to lay up treasure for ourselves in heaven. So let me ask you: How much treasure are you laying up in heaven? When you get to heaven, will you look back on this earth and regret how much treasure you laid up here instead of sending it on ahead to heaven?

A FAITHFUL AND WISE SERVANT?

Just prior to the parable of the talents in Matthew 25, Jesus, in talking about His unexpected return, asks a very pointed question:

> Who then is a faithful and wise servant, whom his master made ruler over his household, to give them food in due season? Blessed is that servant whom his master, when he comes, will find so doing. Assuredly, I say to you that he will make him ruler over all his goods (Matthew 24:45–47).

What a question! "Who then is a faithful and wise servant?" Jesus is asking the same question today. He says that when the master returns, He wants to find His servants doing a good job with the things He has entrusted to them.

When the Lord returns, will He find you being a good and faithful steward? Are you doing the best with what God has given you? Do you know where your money is going every month? Are you tithing, giving, witnessing, and praying?

WHERE IS YOUR HEART?

As we saw earlier in chapter 5, Jesus said: "Therefore if you have not been faithful in the unrighteous mammon, who will commit to your trust the true riches?" (Luke 16:11).

This shows us that God actually uses money to test our hearts; money tests our stewardship and our trustworthiness. It's sobering to think about, but every day God sees the purchases we make and the money we give.

The test is our handling of money. The outcome of that test determines whether He can trust us with true riches or not. That's why, for the Christian, money is more than just a means for buying things. Jesus spent 30 percent of His time teaching on money for a reason.

As Matthew 6:21 shows us, God knows where our heart is by where our treasure is. If your testimony is "My heart is in the kingdom of God," your bank account will either validate or refute that claim.

It's likely that God thinks much more about stewardship than we do. I say that because it's woven throughout the fabric of the Bible.

As we've seen, the first instructions God gave Adam and Eve were stewardship related: Be fruitful, multiply, care for this Garden, and leave that one tree alone! (see Genesis 1:28; 2:17).

The stewardship principle even makes an appearance in the Song of Solomon. There the Shulamite woman says:

> They made me the keeper of the vineyards, but my own vineyard I
> have not kept (Song of Solomon 1:6).

This describes many believers. We can be so busy keeping other people's vineyards—minding their business and trying to tell them how to run their lives—that we don't take care of our own vineyard.

We can't help others if we don't care for what God has given us. If we're not good stewards, it's going to limit our ability to help people and to advance the kingdom of God.

POINTING THE FINGER OF BLAME

God is constant; finances aren't. In other words, finances seem to go up and down, but God is always the same. Every person I know has ups and downs financially. Even people who have a lot of money still have fluctuations in their finances. They have the same opportunities as anyone else to fret, to worry, and to be stressed out about finances.

Sometimes we get upset with God because "He's not coming through for us" financially. We say this even when we didn't pray about whether we were supposed to spend our money the way we did. I'm not trying to sound unkind or harsh, but we need to know that God is not responsible for bills He does not initiate.

We are the ones who are responsible for our finances. *We* are the stewards of our money. We should pray and get God's counsel before we spend money. The truth is that most of the stress, worry, and anxiety in our lives is caused by a failure to exercise good stewardship.

Suppose you have $500 left until payday, and you impulsively choose to spend $300 on a new barbeque grill, leaving you short and in financial trouble. Friend, that's not the judgment of God. That's arithmetic!

Simple subtraction makes that purchase a bad decision with certain consequences. So often we feel like God is punishing us when we're experiencing financial lack. In reality, we're actually punishing ourselves because we didn't take the time to pray about making that purchase or even use good common sense.

> ### Most of the stress, worry, and anxiety in our lives is caused by a failure to exercise good stewardship.

If payday is 10 days away, you have $500 left in your account, and you still have groceries, insurance, electricity, and gasoline to purchase, wisdom and common sense dictate that the grill must wait.

The point is that God frequently gets blamed for our self-inflicted wounds.

Researchers say that the number one reason for divorce is communication, with money following as a close second. When they begin to dig a little deeper, they discover that the number one thing couples don't communicate about is finances. Money is the main source of conflict in marriage.

If we would practice the simple principles of good stewardship, we wouldn't have a lot of the ulcers, headaches, and other health problems associated with financial stress.

GOD WANTS TO BLESS

God truly does desire to bless us. Do you really believe that in your heart of hearts? Let me rephrase the question. Do you believe God desires to curse us? Do you think God desires to do us harm? Of course, you don't!

It's not hard to believe that God isn't out to get us. But many Christians do have a much harder time accepting the fact that God desires to bless them.

Let me state it plainly: God fervently wants to bless us so that we can be a blessing to others. This is exactly what He told Abram in Genesis 12:

> I will make you a great nation; I will bless you and make your name great; and you shall be a blessing (v. 2).

In other words, God's desire was to bless Abram so that he could be a blessing.

The same is true for you and me today. God wants to put great resources in our hands so that we can be conduits of His blessing. Isn't that exactly what we are told in the following New Testament verse?

> And God is able to make all grace abound toward you, that you, always having all sufficiency in all things, may have an abundance for every good work (2 Corinthians 9:8).

God wants us to have an abundance. Why? So that we are ready and able to do every good work. But as we've seen, having abundance is only possible when we are good stewards of the blessings God has given us.

CONFIDENCE IN THE REWARDER

Up to this point, you have heard me repeatedly emphasize the truth that we must not allow *reward* to be our primary motivation for giving—and it is absolutely true.

At the same time, we cannot ignore the fact that God created us to like rewards. It's built into the very fabric of who we are. God created us to respond to rewards because He is a rewarder. In fact, He loves to reward!

That's why I'm not suggesting that it is wrong to believe that God will reward us when we give. Of course, we should expect it. God said it, and He can't lie!

Being confident that God will reward us when we give is simple, childlike faith, but we must be sure we don't allow reward to become the primary motivation for our giving.

When we allow God to do a work in our hearts, the primary motivation becomes giving for the sheer joy of giving, helping for the pure satisfaction of helping and blessing because in doing so we imitate the heavenly Father we love and honor.

By all means, be confident that God will reward you. And unlike my summer camp when I was a kid, God doesn't just wait until the end to have an awards ceremony. He's handing out rewards all the time. And now you know—God rewards good stewardship.

10

NEED, GREED, OR SEED

I t would be impossible to write a Bible-based book on giving without spending some time in 2 Corinthians 9. This is one of the great passages in all of Scripture about the power and blessing that comes through a lifestyle of Spirit-led giving. There are mind-blowing truths there. Here is some background on this chapter.

Paul was about to send a couple of his helpers to the Corinthians to collect a special offering that they had said they wanted to give to the suffering Macedonian church.

In the opening couple of verses, Paul is saying (my paraphrase here), "Guys, you've said that you want to give a generous love offering, and I've been bragging on you to the other churches. Don't embarrass yourselves (and me) by not following through!"

Basically, Paul is commending them for their willingness to give, and he takes the opportunity to teach them some truths about giving.

Paul writes:

> But this I say: He who sows sparingly will also reap sparingly, and he who sows bountifully will also reap bountifully. So let each one give as he purposes in his heart, not grudgingly or of necessity; for God loves a cheerful giver. And God is able to make all grace abound toward you, that you, always having all sufficiency in all things, may have an abundance for every good work (2 Corinthians 9:6–8).

Keep in mind that these words were directed at a group of people who were about to make a sacrificial offering. They were givers.

Paul, writing under the direction of the Holy Spirit, begins by stating the most basic law of giving: "He who sows sparingly will also reap sparingly, and he who sows bountifully will also reap bountifully" (v. 6).

This is the same truth Jesus communicated in Luke 6:38:

> Give, and it will be given to you: good measure, pressed down, shaken together, and running over will be put into your bosom. For with the same measure that you use, it will be measured back to you.

You'll remember that this promise is given not to create our *motivation* for giving but to free us from fear and show us the *reward* of giving.

Paul's very next phrase is an important one. In this verse, we're given the primary guideline for giving. Each person is to give "as he purposes in his heart" (2 Corinthians 9:7).

You are the only person on earth who can decide what the right level of giving is for you. It's between you and the Spirit of God.

Look at this same verse in the *New International Version*:

> Each man should give what he has decided in his heart to give, *not reluctantly or under compulsion, for God loves a cheerful giver* (2 Corinthians 9:7, emphasis added).

God is not looking for tithes, offerings, and gifts that are given "reluctantly or under compulsion." The blessed life is an outgrowth of "cheerful" giving.

> ### *You are the only person on earth who can decide what the right level of giving is for you.*

How do you become a cheerful giver? There is only one way: God must do a work in your heart. As with every other truth we've explored up to this point, it all comes down to the heart.

I learned a valuable lesson about cheerful giving during that remarkable 18-month period in which we gave away nine vehicles. At one point back then, someone who knew we had given away a number of vehicles approached us saying, "We have a spare vehicle and we'd like to anonymously give it to a certain family."

We agreed to take the vehicle and give it to the family, so they transferred the title to our ministry. As I was delivering the car to the recipients' house, the car's engine went out. I had to have the car towed to a garage and pay to have a new engine put in it.

I recall doing a little complaining and grumbling to the Lord about that. I was saying, "Lord, why couldn't the engine have gone out just a few days earlier when those people still had the car—or a few days later after it was delivered to the people who were going to drive it? Why did it go out during the three-day period that it happened to be in my possession?"

I remember the Lord speaking very clearly to me, "I planned it that way, Son. The person who was giving the car away didn't have the money to put a new engine in it, and the family who was receiving the vehicle certainly didn't have the money to do it, but I have blessed you financially. You had the money, and you've acknowledged that it's all My money anyway. I've orchestrated these details perfectly."

Then, the Lord said something else to me, "Son, you should be grateful that I have blessed you financially and that I've blessed you with the privilege of putting a new engine in the vehicle for that family."

And then the Lord gave me a gentle warning, saying, "Now, if you're tired of being a blessing to other people, I can certainly direct those resources to someone else."

Obviously, I repented to the Lord and said, "Father, forgive me. It is all Your money. Thank You for blessing me, and thank You for the opportunity and ability to put a new engine in that vehicle." I quickly went from being a "grudging, under compulsion" giver to being a cheerful one.

Of course, the *natural* state of the human heart is to be a grudging giver. But when we have the heart transplant we talked about in chapter 6, and when we become grateful, unselfish, and generous, only then can we be cheerful givers.

Now, look at the last verse in the 2 Corinthians passage. Notice that Paul said, "God is able" (9:8). This is where every step of faith must begin. You must start by believing that God *is* able. Able to do what? "Make all grace abound toward you" (v. 8).

Let me give you a quick lesson in the nuances and intricacies of the ancient Greek language. The Greek word translated "all" in that verse literally means "all." Isn't that amazing?

You need to know that "God is able to make *all* grace abound toward you" (v. 8, emphasis added). How often? Always! Not sometimes, not on days the stock market closes higher, and not when interest rates are low. Always!

God is able to make all grace abound to you always. When we sow bountifully, God's grace toward us abounds. It overflows.

And what is the result of this overflow of grace? We begin "always having all sufficiency in all things" (v. 8). How much sufficiency? All! (There's that word again.) Sufficiency in how many things? All! (And again.)

This is truly an amazing Scripture. Once you give cheerfully, God is able to make *all* grace abound toward you so that you *always, always* have *all* sufficiency in *all* things. Why? So you may have "an abundance for every good work" (v. 8)!

Verse 8 is a promise that is linked to verses 6 and 7. All grace, abundance, and sufficiency are a direct result of sowing bountifully from a cheerful heart.

NEEDS OR WANTS?

Let me offer a few words about that phrase "all sufficiency" (v. 8). I believe the word "sufficiency" refers to our needs. It relates to having a *sufficient* amount.

Whenever we are about to give a significant offering, it is not unusual to be attacked by fears of insufficiency: Will I have enough? What if I lose my job? What if my car breaks down?

> *Once you give cheerfully, God is able to make*
> all *grace abound toward you so that you* always,
> always *have* all *sufficiency in* all *things.*

Whenever those thoughts come, the first thing to remember is that money is not our sufficiency in the first place—God is our sufficiency. When we begin to put our trust in anything other than God, it is idolatry. It is an idol.

It is precious that God reminds us in this passage that if we give freely and look to Him, we *will* have enough to meet every need. We will have "all sufficiency in all things" (v. 8).

Of course, there is a big difference between a need and a want. Contrary to what some seem to teach, God doesn't promise to satisfy every whim or passing fancy.

Beyond the level called sufficiency is the level called abundance. It is at this level that we're all tested.

It's one thing to have just enough to meet all your needs, but the real heart test comes when we get a little extra. This is the point at which it's possible to pass from need over into greed.

You see this whenever an individual, who has been praying to get out of the bondage of debt, gets an unexpectedly large bonus. Often, it never occurs to this person to take the extra money and pay down their debt. With a little extra money in his hands, he immediately thinks, *Now I can buy something that I really "need"—like that new set of golf clubs!*

This is what I mean when I say that we are tested in our need, and we are tested in our greed. The need test comes as we must trust God to be our sufficiency. The greed test comes when we move beyond sufficiency into abundance.

THE HIGHEST LEVEL

Where using money is concerned, there is a higher level beyond need and greed. The highest use of money is *seed*.

The language Paul used in 2 Corinthians 9:6—"He who sows sparingly will also reap sparingly, and he who sows bountifully will also reap bountifully"—is the language of seed.

How do you view the money you control? Do you see it as being there to meet your need? Is it there to satisfy your greed? Or do you see it as seed?

You'll better understand the truth I'm trying to convey after you've looked at the following Scriptures:

> Remove falsehood and lies far from me; give me neither poverty nor riches—feed me with the food allotted to me; lest I be full and deny You, and say, "Who is the Lord?" Or lest I be poor and steal, and profane the name of my God (Proverbs 30:8-9).

Notice that the writer says, "Give me neither poverty nor riches." This is, basically, need (poverty) or greed (riches). As I have said, this is where we are all tested—in need and greed. The wise author of this proverb understood that. He basically said, "I want to be in the sweet spot of Your provision, Lord."

Is it possible for God to provide for your needs without money? He showed Elijah that He could:

> The ravens brought him bread and meat in the morning, and bread and meat in the evening; and he drank from the brook (1 Kings 17:6).

God didn't need money to provide for Elijah; He only needed some birds. And here's the amazing thing: The birds didn't just bring Elijah dry, old bread. He had steak! Later on, in chapter 19, we see something equally remarkable:

> Then as he [Elijah] lay and slept under a broom tree, suddenly an angel touched him, and said to him, "Arise and eat." Then he looked, and there by his head was a cake baked on coals, and a jar of water. And he went in the strength of that food forty days and forty nights as far as Horeb, the mountain of God (1 Kings 19:5-6, 8).

Cake! The man has angels baking cakes for him! This would be the first known appearance of angel food cake. God not only provided bread and meat but dessert too! That's how good our heavenly Father is.

Without question, God is committed to meeting our needs; but are we committed to using our money as seed?

Think about a farmer who has one sack of seed. He has several options: He could grind the whole sack of seed into flour for bread and then hope that someone would give him some more seed for planting, or he could use some of it for bread and the rest for seed. If he sows that seed, he's going to get a harvest much larger than the original seed sown.

We have already seen Paul use seed as a metaphor for money in 2 Corinthians 9:6. Now look at what he says a few verses later:

> Now may He who supplies seed to the sower, and bread for food, supply and multiply the seed you have sown and increase the fruits of your righteousness, while you are enriched in everything for all liberality, which causes thanksgiving through us to God (2 Corinthians 9:10-11).

Notice that it doesn't say, "God supplies seed to the keeper." He supplies seed to sowers—those who will scatter.

I've heard people say, "Sure, that guy is a giver, but he can afford to be; he's got money." They have it backward. That guy has money *because* he's a giver. God is supplying seed to the sower.

I hate to say this, but some precious people whom God wants to bless will never have money because they won't get their hearts right. God does not supply seed to the keeper and, according to that verse, He does more than just supply seed to the sower:

> He who supplies seed to the sower, and bread for food (v. 10).

God is always mindful of our material needs (so we don't have to be). He wants us to take some of the seed He's given us and eat it, but the rest He wants us to sow. He even adds a promise about that seed:

> [God will] supply and multiply the seed you have sown and increase the fruits of your righteousness (v. 10).

Supply and multiply. God is the only One who can supply our seed; He is also the only One who can multiply it. And when He does, He will also "increase the fruits of your righteousness."

I'm telling you, if you're struggling in some areas of your life, you'll start finding victory when God does a work in this area of your heart.

I believe givers live more righteous lives than takers. Why? Because God, as promised, is increasing the fruits of their righteousness. You're no longer sowing selfishness; you're no longer sowing greed; instead, you're sowing generosity, kindness, and love. As Jesus told us, when you give these things, you will receive them in return, "good measure, pressed down, shaken together, and running over" (Luke 6:38).

That brings me to the three fundamental principles relating to seed that you need to know.

I just made reference to the first one. It is this: You reap what you sow.

LIKE BEGETS LIKE

I know that sounds self-evident, but you would be surprised at how often I observe people expecting things to work some other way in their case.

Embrace this truth: If you sow corn, you're going to reap corn; if you sow wheat, you're going to reap wheat; and if, as Paul suggests, you sow money, you are going to reap money. It's a law that was established at the creation of the world.

> Then God said, "Let the earth bring forth grass, the herb that yields
> seed, and the fruit tree that yields fruit according to its kind, whose
> seed is in itself, on the earth"; and it was so. And the earth brought
> forth grass, the herb that yields seed according to its kind, and the
> tree that yields fruit, whose seed is in itself according to its kind. And
> God saw that it was good (Genesis 1:11–12).

Things multiply after their kind: Like begets like and kind begets kind. Can you imagine a farmer standing in a field in which he has sown wheat seeds and being frustrated because corn is not appearing? That would be foolishness. But that is precisely what so many believers do. They expect a harvest of something they've never planted.

Let me emphasize once again, this is not a holy get-rich-quick scheme. We don't sow for the purpose of getting more money; however, financial growth is a by-product of bountiful sowing. It is a principle: Whatever you sow, you'll reap.

THE RIGHT ORDER

The second principle you need to know about seed is this: You reap *after* you sow.

Once again, I know that seems mind-numbingly simple but you cannot believe how many people say things like, "Someday, when I have more money, I'm going be a giver."

It will never happen. You can't reap *before* you sow. Once again, this a principle God has woven into the natural order of things.

> While the earth remains, seedtime and harvest, cold and heat, winter
> and summer, and day and night shall not cease (Genesis 8:22).

From the very beginning, the order was established. Before there can ever be a harvest, there must be a seedtime. Jesus affirmed this when He said:

> The kingdom of God is as if a man should scatter seed on the ground, and should sleep by night and rise by day, and the seed should sprout and grow, he himself does not know how. For the earth yields crops by itself: first the blade, then the head, after that the full grain in the head. But when the grain ripens, immediately he puts in the sickle, because the harvest has come (Mark 4:26-29).

Imagine the same foolish farmer I mentioned earlier now standing in the field waiting for a crop to come in when he has never planted a seed. "Once this crop comes up, I'm going to do some serious sowing," he says confidently. "I'll be a big-time sower if I ever get this crop to come in."

It is the one who is faithful with the little who will receive much.

Of course, this is absurd. Yet I have heard many believers say pretty much the same thing, such as, "If God will help me close this major business deal, I'm really going to start giving to the church."

It is the one who is faithful with the little who will receive much. You have to start where you are.

MULTIPLICATION

The third principle you should know about seed is this: You reap *more* than you sow. The essence of the message is in the following passage:

> Those who sow in tears shall reap in joy. He who continually goes forth weeping, bearing seed for sowing, shall doubtless come again with rejoicing, bringing his sheaves with him (Psalm 126:5-6).

As this passage implies, the principle of harvest increase is so powerful that, even if you're crying as you scatter your little bag of precious seed, your tears will turn to rejoicing as you begin bringing in your sheaves of harvest.

It's elementary but true, isn't it? In God's kingdom, as in God's natural creation, you reap *more* than you sow.

A couple of kernels of planted seed corn will produce a stalk with several ears. And each ear will contain hundreds of seed kernels (approximately 400 kernels). That's pretty good, isn't it? You always get more when you sow God's way.

A MAN GOD CAN TRUST

I have a friend who, years ago, was making $37,500. At that time, he was consistently giving 10 percent of his gross income. Then the Lord spoke to him and said, *I want you to give 15 percent; and if you will give 15 percent this year, I'll double your income; and, by the way, if you'll give 20 percent the next year, I'll double it again; and if you'll give 25 percent in the year after that, I'll double it again.* He felt very strongly that the Lord had spoken this to his heart.

He did not come back at God and say, *How about this? You double my income, and then I'll start giving 15 percent.*

He took God at His Word and seized the opportunity to stretch his faith and please God. Right away, he started giving 15 percent of his income to the work of the Lord. That year, his income went from $37,500 to $75,000. Taking the Lord at His Word once again, he started giving 20 percent. That following year, he made $150,000. It was at this point that I met him for the first time. We became good friends, and he related this testimony to me.

The next year, he upped his giving to 25 percent, and his income rose to $300,000. I know it sounds incredible, but I know this testimony to be true. This man is a dear friend of mine.

The year after he upped his giving to 30 percent, he made $600,000. A year later, he upped it to 35 percent and grossed $1.2 million. Today, he consistently gives 40 percent of his income to the work of God.

But can I tell you that the greatest thing about this testimony is not how much money my friend gives or makes; it's what God has done in his heart.

This is a man of God. He didn't start giving out of a desire to be rich. He obeyed out of a heart to please God and be used by Him.

God looked down and said, "I need to distribute funds in My kingdom, and here's someone I can trust." And that's precisely what He's looking for. God is looking for people He can trust with wealth.

We must pass the test of need—trusting God to take care of us. We must pass the test of greed—using abundance wisely and in obedience to God's promptings. Moreover, we must pass the test of seed—sowing bountifully—as we observe the three principles of seedtime and harvest.

God can get it to us, if He can only get it through us!

11

GOD REWARDS
GENEROSITY

J oe had a problem, so he took it to his pastor. "Pastor, I'm having trouble tithing these days," he confessed. "What seems to be the hang-up?" his pastor asked. "Well, back when I made $50 a week, I tithed $5, which was easy. And when I made $500 a week, I tithed $50, which was okay. But now that I make $5,000 a week, I'm having a hard time. A $500 tithe is a lot of money! Will you pray for me, Pastor?"

"Sure," said the pastor, "let's pray! Father, please reduce Joe's income back down to $500 a week so that he can honor You with the tithe."

That's a joke, of course. But it's a joke that illustrates a common trap people fall into in their thinking about giving to God. It always makes sense to be generous toward God because He is always generous toward us. Actually, He is *more* than generous in His love toward us—He is extravagant.

I want to show you an account of someone being extravagant in her love toward the Lord:

> Then, six days before the Passover, Jesus came to Bethany, where Lazarus was who had been dead, whom He had raised from the dead. There they made Him a supper; and Martha served, but Lazarus was one of those who sat at the table with Him. *Then Mary took a pound of very costly oil of spikenard, anointed the feet of Jesus,* and wiped His

feet with her hair. And the house was filled with the fragrance of the oil. But one of His disciples, Judas Iscariot, Simon's son, who would betray Him, said, "Why was this fragrant oil not sold for three hundred denarii and given to the poor?" This he said, not that he cared for the poor, but because he was a thief, and had the money box; and he used to take what was put in it. But Jesus said, "Let her alone; she has kept this for the day of My burial. For the poor you have with you always, but Me you do not have always" (John 12:1–8, emphasis added).

What an amazing story! What a graphic contrast of two hearts. On one hand, we have the heart of Mary and, on the other, the heart of Judas. In essence, we have both generosity and selfishness displayed for us in one incident.

Reading it makes me want to ask some questions: Why did Mary do this? Why did she give such an extravagant, generous gift to the Lord? Three hundred denarii was a very large sum of money—basically the equivalent of an entire year's wages. Of course, what constitutes a lot of money is relative. What seems like a lot to me may not seem like much to a multimillionaire. But a year's income is a year's income, no matter who you are.

So, to get a feel for the magnitude of this gift, think about your gross annual income and imagine spending that amount on some perfumed oil. Now, imagine taking it and pouring it onto someone's feet. You are never going to get it back. It's been poured out. All gone! What an extraordinary act. That begs the question, *Why*?

An additional question comes to mind as I read this passage: Why did it bother Judas so much? It wasn't his money.

It highlights the fact that wherever you find generosity, you will find selfishness battling for control. It was true in that situation, and it's true in our own hearts. Each of us has to take a hard, inward look and ask the questions: Am I generous or am I selfish? Which one has the upper hand in my life?

There is a breathtaking selfishness at work in Judas's heart, and it is manifested in his comments about Mary's offering. Look again at the Word of God's commentary on Judas:

> This he said, not that he cared for the poor, but because he was a thief, and had the money box; and he used to take what was put in it (John 12:6).

He didn't care for the poor. He was a thief! Judas pretended to be thinking about others while he was really thinking of no one but himself. This is a tactic that many others down through history have imitated. It is the oldest cover-up for selfishness known to man. That's why it all sounds very familiar.

I once remember riding in the car with someone and passing by the large, beautiful home of a person who I knew to be a committed Christian and who had prospered by following biblical principles and giving generously.

I pointed out the house to my driving companion and mentioned the owner's faith. His response was, "Well, he ought to sell that thing and give the money to the poor." Of course, the person making that comment was living in a house that was nicer than nine-tenths of the world's population could ever dream of owning. And guess what? He had no intention of selling his home and giving the money to Life Outreach International.

The ugly truth is that he didn't care about the poor. He just resented the fact that someone had a nicer house than he did. A spirit of compassion didn't prompt the comment—a spirit of envy did.

This false spirituality manifests itself in several different but similar comments. See if any of these sound familiar: "How could anyone in good conscience drive a car that expensive?" "She sure could have helped a lot of people for what she spent on that coat." Or my personal favorite: "I could sure do a lot of good with the money they spent on that [insert name of luxury item here]." Remarks such as these are pure selfishness and jealousy dressed up as religious superiority—and it's ugly.

This is exactly what Judas did that day. He saw a year's wages being "wasted" instead of passing through his money box so that he could pilfer a good chunk of it. That's basically how Judas viewed a grateful woman's beautiful act of sacrificial worship—a waste.

I have often wondered if, at this point, Judas had realized that Jesus had no intention of establishing an earthly kingdom and making him a "big cheese" in it.

If so, and if he was already working in the background with the religious officials who wanted Jesus dead, it's possible that Judas knew Jesus would soon be killed. In that case, Judas would have assumed that *all* the money in the box would ultimately be his to keep.

Let me give you a contemporary term for that money box. It's the offering box! This money box they carried around held the offerings people gave to support Jesus' ministry. In turn, Jesus would use the money to bless other people—and Judas was stealing from it!

Of course, we think that is outrageous. We can't imagine anyone having the nerve to steal from Jesus. But think about this: In chapter 3, as we dealt with the subject of the tithe, we saw that God rebuked those who were "robbing" Him "in tithes and offerings" (Malachi 3:8).

Is it possible that just as Judas robbed the Lord by taking *out of* the offering box, we have been guilty of robbing Him by failing to put *into* the offering box what is rightfully His in the first place?

I know it sounds hard, but it's very easy for a Christian to operate much more like Judas than Mary.

I suspect Judas was following Jesus for what he thought Jesus could do for him. As a member of the anti-Roman Zealot Party, he was looking for a prominent position in the new kingdom that would throw off the shackles of Rome. Of course, so were most of the other disciples, as their frequent jockeying for position showed.

But more than anyone else, Judas was hanging out with Jesus based on the What's In It For Me? (W.I.I.F.M.) principle. And as soon as it became clear to Judas that Jesus wasn't going to come through in the way he had hoped, he betrayed Him.

Of course, that's not too different from what many people do today. They follow God out of the W.I.I.F.M. principle instead of being focused on what they can do for Him. And as soon as He "disappoints" them—when He doesn't come through for them in the way they want—they get upset and quit coming to church.

Selfishness, by its very nature, cares about nothing and no one but self. A selfish person will sell out his or her friends if it will help the person get what he or she wants. And a selfish person will always, always find good reasons not to be generous.

That's exactly what Judas did. "Hey, don't blow that expensive perfume on Jesus. We can turn it into cash and give the money to the poor!"

As Judas did, selfishness tries to get the focus off of the selfish one and onto the "extravagance" of others. Selfishness drives by nice houses and criticizes other people's blessings. Selfishness always looks after self by pointing at someone else.

CONFRONTING YOUR WEAKNESS

Who gave Judas the responsibility of carrying the money box? Jesus, of course. Now, ask yourself, did Jesus know that Judas was a thief when He gave him that responsibility? Certainly! That brings me to another important lesson from this story.

This is a startling revelation for many Christians, but we will always be tempted in the area of our weakness. As a matter of fact, just as Judas—the guy with the weakness for money and prestige—was given responsibility for the money box, God will give you responsibility in the area of *your* weakness.

Why? you may be thinking. *Does God set us up to fail?* No! Actually, He's setting us up to succeed. The only way we can truly succeed is by confronting our weaknesses and overcoming them.

When God gives you some small responsibility in the area of your weakness, He is taking you through a growth process necessary for your success. You see:

> No temptation has overtaken you except such as is common to man; but God is faithful, who will not allow you to be tempted beyond what you are able (1 Corinthians 10:13).

According to the Bible, you have never experienced a temptation that you did not have the ability to resist. We always make a conscious choice to sin. However, God wants to help us turn our area of greatest potential for defeat into our area of greatest victory.

Thus, Jesus gives a thief responsibility for the money and, in doing so, gives him the opportunity to overcome his selfishness and greed. But Judas didn't do it, did he?

We will always be tempted in the area of our weakness.

Money is a bigger test than you think. In fact, you are being tested by money right now. It is vital that you understand this truth: The extent of the responsibility you will have in the kingdom is directly proportional to how you handle money.

If you doubt the truth of this statement, take a fresh look at Jesus' words in Luke 16:

> Therefore if you have not been faithful in the unrighteous mammon, who will commit to your trust the true riches? And if you have not been faithful in what is another man's, who will give you what is your own? (vv. 11–12).

You are being tested right now. The prize for passing the test is true riches. But, then, what are true riches?

True riches are people—the privilege of seeing those you love saved, made whole, and growing in God. True riches are the words of knowledge, gifts of healing, faith, and miracles that minister to people.

True riches are being able to help others who have spent their entire lives in bondage to depression or oppression experience freedom for the first time. True riches are souls.

Please know that I don't want to sound harsh, but I must tell you the truth. God isn't going to give you responsibility in the kingdom of God or even the house of God if you can't even handle your finances. He cannot!

As a pastor, I deliberately follow God's example. This may shock some people, but I will never give a person a leadership position in the church if he or she can't handle money.

I know I'm going to give an account to God for the sheep in the flock I've been charged with leading. The Bible says undershepherds will give an account to the Chief Shepherd (Jesus) about how they cared for and protected the sheep. That's why I will never delegate responsibility over precious sheep to someone if they can't even handle personal finances in a biblical way.

Mary came to Jesus with a heart overflowing with gratitude and love. That love translated itself into worship through an offering of great price.

In a similar way, we show God each week how full of gratitude and love our hearts are. So ask yourself some revealing questions: What do your offerings say about your heart levels of gratitude and love for God? What does your spending say about what's truly important to you on this earth?

Judas wanted to keep everything he could in order to build his own kingdom. Mary was willing to give everything she had in order to bless the King.

EXTRAVAGANCE FOR GOD

As I've said, there is a battle going on inside each of us. It is a battle between self-ishness and generosity, and it is a battle generosity must win.

Let me tell you something about generosity that will help you recognize it when you see it: Generosity is extravagant. One year's wages came pouring out of Mary's container that day. Surely, that was an extravagant gift to the Lord. But how do we evaluate what constitutes an extravagant gift today?

Now, before you answer that, let's just remind ourselves of something. God owns everything. All the wealth of heaven and earth are His. Right? So, what size gift would impress God? Is $1 million an extravagant gift to Him? Is a $100 billion gift extravagant to God? How is it even possible to give an extravagant gift to the God of the universe?

There is only one thing you can possibly give to God that would constitute an extravagant gift—yourself. You can offer up all you are and ever will be. Now, that's an extravagant gift. That is really what Mary was doing that day. The perfumed oil was just a symbol—a token—representing the fact that all of her heart was the Lord's. That was the extravagant gift Mary gave that day.

It's a gift that a selfish-hearted person like Judas could never hope to give or even understand.

THE LADDER OF GIVING

As of this writing, I've been preaching on giving for about 30 years. But about 13 years ago, I saw something about giving that I had never before seen in the Word. I saw that for the Christian, there are actually three levels of giving to the Lord.

I will elaborate shortly, but I will tell you what they are right now. There are three levels of giving to the Lord:

1. Tithes

2. Offerings

3. Extravagant Offerings

Soon after making what I thought was this breakthrough discovery, I excitedly called a friend of mine, a person with a strong gift of giving—to share it with him.

Over the phone I said, "The Lord has shown me something I've never seen before. Did you know that there are three levels of giving?" Very matter-of-factly, he said, "Yes, I did, and I can even tell you what they are."

I remember thinking, *Wrong, Mr. Smarty Pants. I just got this fresh from heaven. I've never heard it preached or taught at any time. There is no way you know what I'm about to say.* So I called his bluff. "All right, then, what are they?" He said, "Tithes, offerings, and painful offerings."

He had phrased it a little less delicately than I had, but that was it! He knew! (I should have known that a mature believer who functions in the gift of giving would have already received this revelation.)

Sadly, most believers never even get to the first level. Every study done indicates that only a small fraction of people who claim the name of Christ even tithe consistently.

I find it mind-boggling, but the truth is that most believers struggle with tithing. Are you ever surprised in January, when you get your annual giving record from your church, at the percentage of your gross income that you have given? Most people are. Many people who *intend* to tithe and think they are, actually aren't!

As I said, very few believers ever get to the first rung of the ladder of giving; consequently, they never even get a glimpse of the joy, fun, and blessing available at the higher levels.

Many people who intend *to tithe and think they are, actually aren't!*

However, over the years, I have observed that those who do get to the first level usually move on to the next one. Why? Because tithing removes the curse and opens the windows of heaven over us. So, if we ever start tithing, we're much more likely to start giving offerings as the Lord leads us.

Nevertheless, very few Christians will ever reach the third level of giving to the Lord—the level of extravagant giving—and this is a tragedy. I'm so saddened when I think about the fact that so many believers will never taste the joy of giving an extravagant offering to the Lord. But you can, just as many of the most remarkable figures of the Bible did.

For instance, King David gave an extravagant offering to the Lord to pave the way for the building of the Temple by his son Solomon. Do you know how much of his own money David set aside for the building of the Temple? Converted to today's currency, it would be $21 billion. That's an extravagant gift, even for a king.

Here's another of the Bible's extravagant gifts: David's son Solomon became known around the world as extremely wise. Do you remember how Solomon received that wisdom? (See 1 Kings 3.)

Solomon had just been set in as king. According to tradition, he was supposed to go offer an offering to the Lord. He was to sacrifice a bull. On the appointed day, do you know what Solomon did? He sacrificed 1,000 bulls.

Can't you hear his advisors? "Uh ... listen ... we know you're new and everything, but ... uh ... didn't you know that you are only supposed to offer one offering? But, hey, we know you're excited, so if you want to get extravagant, why not sacrifice 10 ... or even 100? But 1,000? Think about it, Solomon ... we'll be here all night!"

Solomon personally gave 1,000 bulls that day. And that night, God came to him and said, "Ask anything, and I'll give it to you."

Do you know why God said "Ask anything of Me"? It is because Solomon had demonstrated that his heart was generous, not selfish. Solomon was a giver.

I can assure you that a person who is not a giver at the highest level is not likely to have God come to him and say, "Ask anything." He can't, because He hasn't had the opportunity to do a work in that heart. He could not trust him with the blank check He handed to Solomon.

Let me tell you about another extravagant gift in the Bible. It is one that rivals that of David and Solomon combined. We find it in Luke 21:

And He [Jesus] saw also a certain poor widow putting in two mites (v. 2).

That's right. A poor widow with her offering of two mites made the extravagant gift list because, according to Jesus, it was all she had. It took as much—or more—faith for her to give two mites as it did for David to give $21 billion in gold! It is not the amount; it is the heart. Two pennies constitute an extravagant gift when it is all you have.

Here's another extravagant gift recorded in the Bible: On a remote hilltop in what would one day become Jerusalem, a man named Abraham prepared to offer up his only, miraculous son (see Genesis 22). I'd call that extravagant.

I'll give you one even better than that: Not too far away from that hilltop 2,000 years later, God Himself offered His only, blameless Son as a sacrifice for our freedom and lives. I'd call that an extravagant gift. I'd also call that a painful gift.

God is the ultimate extravagant giver. He is generous, and He wants to do a work in our hearts that makes us more like Him.

A PURPOSE FOR EVERY GIFT

As we have seen, the biblical account of Mary's extravagant gift is recorded in John 12. If you want a little insight into what made her an extravagant giver, you only have to back up one chapter.

Do you remember what happened in John 11? Jesus raised Mary and Martha's brother Lazarus from the dead. One chapter later, Mary gave her most precious possession to the Lord.

Is it possible that the events of chapter 11 gave Mary a new perspective? Could burying her beloved brother, having him lie in the grave for four days, and then suddenly seeing him restored to life at the Word of Jesus have changed Mary's values and priorities? Maybe material possessions didn't seem so precious anymore.

Getting a glimpse of what Jesus can do for the people we love has a way of doing that for us.

Perhaps our perspective needs to change as well. After all, if you know Jesus, you've been raised from the dead yourself.

> But God, who is rich in mercy, because of His great love with which He loved us, even when we were dead in trespasses, made us alive together with Christ (by grace you have been saved), and raised us up together, and made us sit together in the heavenly places in Christ Jesus (Ephesians 2:4–6).

Shouldn't we have the same perspective Mary had? You see, a generous heart stems from a grateful heart.

Matthew and Mark also record the account of Mary's extravagant gift. In fact, they depict Mary pouring the oil on Jesus' head as well as His feet. Mark also records some words of Jesus that John didn't. After Judas complained about the "waste" of the precious oil, Jesus responded by saying:

> She has done what she could. She has come beforehand to anoint My body for burial (Mark 14:8).

If you recall the details of the crucifixion, you will remember that Jesus' body was taken off the cross just before the Sabbath was about to begin at sundown. That meant they had to quickly wrap Jesus' body in cloth and lay Him in the tomb.

There was no time to anoint His body with perfumed oils or spices as they normally would. In fact, it was this problem that a group of women were coming to rectify three days later when they encountered the angels who told them that Jesus had risen (see Luke 24:1-5).

Think about it: The only person on earth who received the privilege of anointing Jesus' body for burial was Mary. She didn't know that was what she was doing until Jesus said, "She has come beforehand to anoint My body for burial" (Mark 14:8).

Sometimes, when we give obediently and extravagantly at the prompting of the Spirit, we have no idea how significant that gift really is; but God knows. God has a purpose for every gift.

When I think about that truth, I am reminded of some friends of mine. Thirty years ago, they were newly married, deeply in love, and flat broke—no money, no savings, nothing.

In their first year of marriage, my friend got a surprise bonus check from his job. It was the largest amount of money they had ever seen in one lump sum. To them, it was a huge amount, especially since they didn't really have anything.

As soon as the initial euphoria subsided, they started sensing that, even though they had lots of needs and plenty of ways to spend the windfall, somehow the money wasn't for them. (These people have generous hearts.)

They went to the pastor of the church and said, "We don't know specifically who or what this is for, but we want to give this money." Then their pastor said, "Yesterday, I met with a widow in our church. I found out they are going to take her house if she can't come up with a certain amount of money. The amount she needs, to the penny, is the amount of this check."

God has a purpose for every gift.

UNAVOIDABLE REWARDS

There is one more thing I want you to know about generosity: It is rewarded.

According to Matthew 26, Jesus made an interesting comment after He heard Judas giving Mary a hard time for being extravagant.

> But when Jesus was aware of it, He said to them, "Why do you trouble the woman? For she has done a good work for Me. For you have the poor with you always, but Me you do not have always. For in pouring this fragrant oil on My body, she did it for My burial. *Assuredly, I say to you, wherever this gospel is preached in the whole world, what this woman has done will also be told as a memorial to her*" (vv. 10-13, emphasis added).

When Mary approached Jesus to anoint Him with her oil, I doubt she was saying to herself, *I'll bet this is going to make me world-famous. They'll be talking about this for years!* She was just thinking about giving and how much she wanted to express her love for Jesus.

Generosity doesn't give to receive, but generosity is *always* rewarded by God. If you give, God is going to bless you. No power on earth can stop it. I'm sorry if that bothers you. You're just going to have to deal with it. I know you're just giving to give. I realize you're not giving to receive. Nonetheless, blessing is the by-product of giving. That's just the way it is. You can't get out of it!

To do otherwise, God would have to violate His own nature. God is a rewarder. We saw that in Hebrews 11. Like any good parent, God desires to reward His children.

Remember the friend of mine who annoyingly knew the three levels of giving before I could enlighten him? One evening several years ago, he was going over his bills and finances. Like many people, he uses a computer program to track his spending and account balances. When all his bills were paid, he saw that he still had a very healthy balance in his checking account. With a grateful heart, he prayed, *Lord, You've really blessed me. It's amazing to have that much money in my checking account. Thank You.* That made him curious about how much money he had in his other accounts.

So he checked his savings balance and saw a very large sum there as well. Once again, he prayed, *Lord, You have been so good. Your blessings are just awesome. Thank You.*

It made him wonder how much money he had altogether. He looked at his investment account and his retirement account too. Then he added everything up and got a number.

As he went to bed that night, he knew in dollars and cents exactly how much cash he had, and it was an amazing amount of money. He drifted off to sleep that night with his heart full of thanksgiving and wonder.

The next morning, as he was praying in his quiet time, he heard the voice of the Lord ask him, "How much money do you have?" Immediately, he thought, *Uh-oh. I'm in trouble now. I never should have added up those accounts. Counting got King David in trouble too!*

Of course, he knew, to the penny, how much money he had. He had gone to a lot of trouble the night before to find out his net worth. Although he knew better, he tried to weasel. "Well, Lord ... uh ... What do You mean? ... Do You mean how much money do I have in my wallet?" Again the question came, "How much money do you have?" My friend responded, "How much do I have in my checking account? Is that what You mean?" The question came again, "How much money do you have?"

Finally, he said, "Lord, You know I added it up last night. This is how much money I have," and he quoted the figure. Then the Lord said, "Would you give it to Me?"

At that point, my friend said that he had a moment of disbelief. *This can't be happening. This is unbelievable. God is asking me to give away all the money I've spent the last 20 years accumulating.* But then remembering, as people with the gift of giving are likely to do, that it all belongs to God, he felt an overwhelming sense of joy and excitement rise up within him. It was unspeakable joy. "Lord," he responded, "I would love to give it to You." And so he did it. He gave away every penny that he had as the Lord led him.

Over the next 12 months, God blessed his business to a degree that he had never seen before. One year after giving away all the money he had, this man had more than what he had given. In that one year, he accumulated more than he had in 20 years of hard work and saving. Every account was not only replenished but had grown. What took him 20 years to do, God did in only one. Generosity toward God is always rewarded.

WHEN YOU GIVE EXTRAVAGANTLY

Let me close this chapter by telling you what almost always happens when the Spirit of God speaks to you about an extravagant gift.

The first step in giving an extravagant gift to the Lord is *hearing*. You don't give extravagant gifts out of your own thinking or planning. You need to hear God.

Hearing from God isn't hard or complicated. The Spirit wants you to know God's will and ways. He is always speaking. The voice of the Spirit is rarely a loud or booming voice. It's usually a very soft impression. And, frankly, you can talk yourself out of it.

The second phase is *excitement*. Once you hear from God about a significant gift, it's natural to get extremely excited. This excitement doesn't last indefinitely, however.

It almost always gives way to phase three: *fear*. Like my friend, you are most likely going to have thoughts that shout: *This is crazy! This is absolutely crazy!* The fact is that almost everything in the Christian life seems crazy to the natural mind.

After fear, comes phase four of giving an extravagant gift: *logic*. In the logic phase, you'll start thinking of lots of reasons you shouldn't do what you've heard God say. You will think of lots of alternative plans and programs.

Do you think Abram had to wrestle with logic when God asked him to offer his son Isaac? Do you think logic might have had a thing or two to say to Peter before he stepped out of that boat?

I'm not saying logic is wrong. I am saying that if logic says one thing and God's voice says something else, God's voice wins.

Invariably, after logic comes *doubt*. Did I really hear God correctly? Maybe that was just my overactive imagination. What if it was the devil?!!!

The devil always overplays his hand because, at that point, you can ask yourself, *Would the devil really try to get me to give money to the preaching of the gospel so that more people will get saved? I don't think so!*

That's when you move into the final phase leading up to an extravagant gift: *faith*. Once you get back to faith, the excitement returns, and that's when you can follow through and obey.

Ask yourself this question: *Am I generous, or is selfishness still the dominant force in my heart?*

How much of you does God have? Does He have all of you? Does He have your dreams? Your desires? Your possessions?

God wants to do a work in our hearts. He wants to make us generous.

12

GUARANTEED
FINANCIAL RESULTS

U p to this point, I've highlighted some key biblical truths about giving, stewardship, and what it really means to live the blessed life. I have reinforced the presentation of those truths with numerous testimonies (mine and others) that depict these principles in glorious action.

In this closing chapter, I want to show you how these truths, faithfully applied, will produce guaranteed financial results for you. That's right, I said, "Guaranteed financial results." I have chosen those words carefully and deliberately.

Of course, in the world's economic system, there is no such thing as guaranteed results. Advertisements for investment opportunities are required by law to point out to you that past performance is not an indicator of future results.

Nevertheless, I can tell you without hesitation that if you will apply the principles I've outlined in these chapters, you will get remarkable, positive financial results—guaranteed!

The reason I can say that is because God is faithful. His past performance *is* an indicator of future results. As we've seen repeatedly, whenever God's people are obedient and faithful, God blesses.

I want to remind you of the central truth of this book. Giving is important because it does a supernatural work in our hearts, and that's what God is after—our hearts. God is not after our money. He doesn't need it. But our treasure is tied to our hearts. Thus, God goes *through* our treasure to get to our hearts. That's why I can promise you "guaranteed financial results." When you give with a heart transformed by God, the results are guaranteed. God will back up His Word.

God is not a man that He should lie. He simply cannot do so without violating His very nature, which holds the universe together.

When God makes a promise, He will fulfill His promise as we fulfill the conditions of that promise. An example of a promise with a condition is "Whosoever shall call on the name of the Lord shall be saved" (Acts 2:21; see also Joel 2:32, KJV). Salvation is a promise that God faithfully keeps for anyone who fulfills the condition of that promise—calling upon the name of the Lord.

We find another great conditional promise in 2 Chronicles 16:

> The eyes of the Lord search the whole earth in order to strengthen those whose hearts are fully committed to him (v. 9, NLT).

In other words, God is searching and searching for generous hearts—hearts He knows He can trust with wealth and resources.

God has all the resources of the universe at His disposal. At the same time, He sees poor people who need to be fed, willing missionaries who need to be equipped and sent, and churches that need to be built. That's why His eyes are roaming earth, looking for faithful-hearted stewards through whom He can channel millions of dollars into His kingdom.

Do you have such a heart? I can assure you that if you become a conduit for the funds God wants to channel to others, you and your family will be well taken care of by God. As we just read, God is looking to strongly support such individuals.

God is after our hearts, and the evidence that He has our hearts is this: We give simply to give rather than giving to receive; and we give because we want to bless people, help people, and enlarge the kingdom of God. This, rather than reward, is our primary motive.

This is the great paradox of living the blessed life: When we give without thought to whether or not we will receive, then we receive.

Of course, the rewards do come. We have seen this truth throughout the Word and in all of the testimonies I've shared. When we give out of transformed hearts, God is going to bless us so that we can give even more. Good stewards are entrusted with more. Faithful servants receive true riches.

I know it seems like a catch-22. This is the great paradox of living the blessed life: When we give without thought to whether or not we will receive, then we receive (good measure, pressed down, shaken together, and running over). In other words, when our motive for giving is right, God will reward us for giving.

This is the vital truth I see left out of many of the teachings on giving. All we hear is "Give, and God will bless you." But what about our hearts? What about selfishness? What about greed? Isn't God trying to work those things out of our lives? Absolutely.

But when we come to the place where we say, "Lord, I just want to give to You because I love You," God responds by saying the same thing in return: "I give and bless you because I love you and because you've shown I can trust you with resources."

It's like the childhood game of tag we used to play. It seemed to me that I was always it. I would run and run until I finally caught someone, and as soon as I touched him or her, that person would turn around quickly and touch me back, and I would be it again. That's why I always wanted to enforce the rule of no touchbacks.

Well, when it comes to blessing and giving, God never practices no touchbacks. We can be glad to know that God is all about touching back. He is all about returning and reciprocating. When I touch God, He immediately touches me back.

This is one of the things that I love about worship, because in worship I touch Him and He touches me back. But it's the same in giving. As soon as I give with the right heart and the right motive, God gives back to me. Then I have even more to give.

God wants to reward us, just as we want to reward our children when they do the right thing with the right attitude. Don't we long to see an attitude of kindness, love, and compassion in our children?

The trap the enemy wants us to fall into is worshipping the blessings rather than the Blessor. Satan wants us to focus on the blessings that God has given us. We fall into that subtle trap when we begin seeking after the blessings that come from God's hand rather than seeking God's face. We can never allow the blessings to have our hearts. Our hearts must be wholly God's.

Nevertheless, when we give with pure motives and hearts for God, He will immediately reward us and increase us so that we can give even more. That's why I can say with confidence that the financial results of giving are guaranteed. They are backed by the full faith and credit of the Word of God.

Yes, we are laying up treasure in heaven, but God also guarantees us financial results on earth when we give with pure hearts. God is the only One who can truly give us this revelation, and God is the only One who can truly do this work in our hearts.

God can change us from takers into givers. We were all born takers; we are born-again givers. Now it's our responsibility to renew our minds. God wants us to be generous, gracious, kindhearted, and compassionate. When God does that work in our hearts—when we begin to give simply because we want to—then we actually will be rewarded so that we can give even more to the kingdom of God.

WHATEVER HE SAYS

I have shared this message in many churches over the years, and recently, as the senior pastor of Gateway Church in Southlake, Texas, it has been my privilege to share these truths with our members there.

I have shared this message to our congregation several times over the years. As I write, almost 15 years have passed since our very first service. Since then, the Lord has increased our numbers dramatically. Today, we are a diverse church with more than 36,000 active members.

Time and again, I have watched as people in our church catch this revelation. God changes their hearts, and they come to the altar with tears, wanting to give. They come to give rather than receive. They give simply to give, and God richly blesses them as a result.

During the preparation and writing of this book, our church began the construction of our first building. We had a strong desire to build without debt, if possible, and so as a church, we had set aside a weekend for a miracle offering.

Now we called it a miracle offering not because we wanted to see a miraculous amount of money come in but because we wanted to see God do a miracle in our hearts. Our staff and lay leadership longed to see God take us to a new level of selflessness and generosity. We wanted to be changed from takers into givers. The Lord directed us to designate this offering as an opportunity for Him to do that kind of miracle in us.

That's why I asked people to give the largest possible gift they could give. I encouraged what we described in the previous chapter as an extravagant gift to the Lord.

When the wise men came to Jesus, they didn't bring small gifts; they brought extravagant gifts because they wanted to worship the Lord.

I knew that, as the pastor, I wasn't exempt from this call to extravagant giving. On the contrary, there is no way I could expect our people to do something I wasn't willing to do myself. So my wife and I began to pray about what we were to give.

One week before the scheduled miracle-offering weekend, Pastor Jimmy Evans from Trinity Fellowship Church in Amarillo ministered in our weekend services. Trinity Fellowship was instrumental in planting our church, and Jimmy Evans has been powerfully used by God as a mentor to me and as an apostle to our body.

That weekend, Jimmy preached a wonderful message titled, "What Mary Knew About Miracles." It was taken from John 2, where Jesus does His very first miracle (turning water into wine) in the presence of His mother, Mary. Pastor Jimmy centered his message on the instruction Mary gave the servants at the wedding, "Whatever He says to you, do it" (John 2:5).

He rightly pointed out that this instruction is basically the key to receiving a miracle from the Lord. Whatever Jesus says to you—do it! This certainly applies to financial miracles too. When it comes to giving, whatever He says—do it. If He says, *Give $1,000*—do it. If He says, *Give $100,000*—do it.

Jesus took what they had in the natural (water) and turned it into something supernatural (miracle wine). That's what God does with our finances. He takes what is natural and turns it into something supernatural.

Whatever Jesus says to you—do it!

Whatever He says—do it. It's the key. This is basically the same principle I described earlier in this book as the IO (Instant Obedience) Principle. As soon as you hear God say it—do it.

The following week, with the principle involved in the water into wine miracle in Cana firmly established in our minds, we placed large water pots at the front of the sanctuary to serve as offering baskets.

After I preached that day, I watched people come forward to place their extravagant offerings to the Lord in those earthen water pots. I watched many couples and individuals stand there, with tears streaming down their faces, praying and consecrating themselves and their offerings to God. It was a serious convocation that day.

I watched as people's hearts were broken and changed. I saw ties to the temporal things of this world cut as God's people freely invested in the eternal. I watched joy flood souls who had just received the revelation that we can send our treasure on ahead rather than leaving it on this earth.

I saw families that I knew were going through difficult times come forward saying, "Father, in faith, we're going to acknowledge that You are Lord and that even in this situation, we're going to trust You to work a miracle in our family."

In the weeks and months that have followed that remarkable weekend, the testimonies have flowed in consistently. In family after family, God showed Himself faithful to reward cheerful, thankful, generous givers.

And one of the many testimonies to come out of that weekend is mine.

A FRESH WORK IN MY HEART

About a month before our miracle-offering weekend, I was ministering at Calvary Assembly in Orlando, Florida—the church of my good friend Pastor Clark Whitten. At offering time that night, Pastor Whitten stood before the congregation and said, "There's a blessing on this offering tonight."

Now I know Clark Whitten, and I know that he doesn't make that kind of pronouncement lightly or manipulatively. When he said, "There's a blessing on this offering tonight," he was speaking prophetically by the Spirit of God, and I knew it.

When I heard that, I thought to myself, *Well, if there's a blessing, I'm going to give everything that I can. I want the money I give to be blessed and have the greatest impact for the kingdom.*

As that thought went through my mind, I heard the Lord say to me, "There's a blessing on the miracle offering that your church is about to give also." At that moment, I knew what the Lord wanted Debbie and me to do. He wanted us to empty every account we had and give it to the Lord—checking accounts, savings, money market accounts, even our retirement account—everything.

As I have mentioned previously, there have been several occasions when God has prompted us to give away essentially all the money we had; however, most of those occasions were early in our married life. I don't mean to minimize what we did back then. Each time, it required a huge leap of faith on our part. But as you may have noticed, it does seem that as we get older, the stakes get higher and things get more complicated.

I knew God was directing us, though, because my immediate response wasn't fear or reluctance. On the contrary, I got very excited in my heart. Of course, it's one thing for *me* to hear from God that we should give away every cent we have; it's another thing for my wife to hear it. And so I went to Debbie and said, "Honey, I think I know what the Lord wants us to do for the miracle offering." "What is that?" she asked. So I told her what the Lord had said. Would you like to know what her response was? "I think that's the most exciting thing I've heard in a long time." That was my confirmation. She was excited about it, and so was I.

Several weeks later, the time had come to follow through. At our church, we have Saturday evening services as well as Sunday morning services. That Saturday evening of the miracle-offering weekend, Debbie and I went down to one of those big water pots with a check for every penny that we had. We had liquidated everything. We placed our check in the offering with great excitement. We have learned through the years that when God asks you to do something extraordinary, it's because He wants to do something extraordinary.

During morning worship the next day, the Lord spoke something to me that affected me profoundly. From time to time, when I stand before my congregation to preach, I will jokingly ask, "How many of you would rather be here in church this morning than in jail?" It's just a lighthearted way to start the service. Well, as we sang that morning, the Lord asked me the same question—only He was serious. The Holy Spirit said, "Would you rather be here than in jail?"

Then He reminded me of the road I was on before Jesus came into my life. I didn't give my life to Jesus until I was 19 years old. Prior to that day, I was involved in some very bad things. In that moment, the Lord showed me the life from which He had saved me. He gently reminded me of how gracious He has been to me. As He did, I began to weep. I cried all through worship and right up to the point when I was supposed to get up and preach. As I stood before my congregation, I was still a mess.

The most precious and lasting blessings that come are often the ones no one can see.

As I have tried to point out in every way I possibly can in this book, God does a work in our hearts when we give. Once again, that weekend, our extravagant gift had opened the door for God to do a deep, deep work of gratitude in my heart, and I wouldn't trade that work for all the money in the world.

Yes, God rewards and blesses us when we give. However, the most precious and lasting blessings that come are often the ones no one can see.

THE REST OF THE STORY

Less than six weeks from the day Debbie and I gave every penny we had, God, by His grace, restored it all and then some. Think about it: Within 40 days, we found ourselves with more money than we had before giving it all away in that one offering. It was supernatural. God guarantees financial results. He's the only One who can.

Giving when the Lord leads, helping people know the love and goodness of God, keeping the focus on God rather than on things, being generous, and allowing God to do a work in our hearts are the keys to making our journey on earth an adventure of joy and purpose.

These are the keys to *the blessed life.*

AFTERWORD: GOD'S ROAD MAP FOR A BLESSED LIFE

G od's road map to living a blessed life is revealed from Genesis through Revelation. Each signpost along the way marks a new depth of understanding for how to apply His principles to our daily lives. It is in His timing and according to His plan that we learn to negotiate the curves and bumps in the road that takes us higher up the mountain toward fulfilling our God-given destinies.

This process unfolds one step at a time, just as a book unfolds one chapter at a time. Every author will tell you that a book is never truly finished—as soon as it hits the press, there is another revelation that you know should have been included. That's exactly what happened when *The Blessed Life* was first published. Usually an author just saves the addition to put in his next book, but I strongly felt that this Afterword needed to be added to *The Blessed Life* as it goes into its next printing.

A HEART FOR ISRAEL

Understanding that God is concerned for the Jewish people (as each believer needs to be) and that His road map has a prescribed order is paramount to the successful application of the principles of giving outlined in the chapters of this book. This is not just for our personal reward but also for the fulfillment of God's kingdom purposes in these critical days. Before you read any further, I want you to ask yourself, "Am I concerned for the Jewish people?" Be honest, because this is a heart issue. God has dealt with my heart in a new way, and He may be asking you to change your heart as you read further.

Let me tell you where I've come from in my love for Israel. I'm going to share with you what I believe God has called us to do.

One morning in the early 1990s during my quiet time, I asked God where He wanted me to read in the Bible. He said, "Psalm 122." As I read verse 6, suddenly He said, "Pray for the peace of Jerusalem." As I began to pray, I found myself praying for the Church. God quickly stopped me and said, "No, I said pray for Jerusalem—it's not the same thing."

You see, a false doctrine called *replacement theology* has crept into the Church, which says that the Church has replaced Israel. This deception cannot be backed up by Scripture. Believers in Christ have not replaced Israel. Rather, we—as Gentiles who believe in Jesus—have been grafted into the commonwealth of believing Israel. *We are now citizens of Israel.* This truth has very different implications than the false teaching of replacement theology. If you don't see that, you'll miss the meaning of God's wonderful promises to His people. If God is not going to keep His promises to the Jewish people, why would He keep His promises to us? God is either a promise-keeping God or He isn't.

Read Jeremiah, Ezekiel, Isaiah, Romans, and Ephesians, and you'll understand that there is a land and a people called Israel that were chosen by God. They were not chosen because they were special—God said, "I did not choose you because you are special or because you are the largest nation" (Deuteronomy 7:7). Israel is smaller than the U.S. state of Rhode Island, and God chose tiny Israel for this very reason. He knew that if the smallest could become the strongest, then the rest of the world would know that their God is the true God. This doesn't mean that the Jewish people are more important to God than other people—it means that they are part of God's plan in history, of which we are a part today. Satan understands the plan, and that's why he has tried to convince the Church to hate Jews for hundreds of years.

God's plan is the reason He put it in my heart to pray for the peace of Jerusalem. He is concerned for the Jewish people, and He wants me to be concerned as well. As I began to pray that morning, an overwhelming burden for God's people came over me like I had never felt before. It was totally unexpected.

We had an elders' meeting at the church later that day. At the time, I was an associate pastor and elder at Shady Grove Church in Grand Prairie, Texas. Our regular meetings usually started about nine in the morning and finished at noon, followed by lunch together—but God had a different and unexpected agenda that day. During our prayer time, someone started praying for Israel, and just as it had happened earlier in the morning, I felt a tremendous burden. I began to pray, and then another elder, Wayne Wilks (who has since founded the Messianic Jewish Bible Institute), shared from the Scriptures in Ezekiel, Isaiah, and Jeremiah.

The meeting lasted until 5:00 pm that day. We conducted no business. All we did was read the Scriptures about Israel and pray. It was truly a "God thing." My heart changed and my eyes were opened.

As believers, God is always opening new truths to us. They aren't actually *new*—they've been in the Scriptures all along—but they are new to us. Many people experience this God-given enlightenment when they suddenly understand the gifts of the Spirit or baptism in the Spirit or deliverance and overcoming the enemy. In the same way, once your eyes are opened to God's deep love and concern for Israel, you will see it throughout Scripture and understand how it is closely tied to what God is doing in the world. That's what happened for me that day. I saw God's plan.

Before that meeting, our eldership had been praying for a divine plan to reach Muslims with the gospel. As we prayed, Wayne showed us in Romans 11:15 that when the Jewish people accept their Messiah, a worldwide revival will break out. We read in Ezekiel 36 that "the nations will know that I am the Lord ... when I show myself holy through [Israel] before their eyes" (v. 23). The phrase "the nations around you" appears three times in that chapter, and it dawned on us that the nations around Israel are predominantly Islamic. God had given us the answer to our prayers for reaching Muslims with the gospel.

GOD'S ORDER: "TO THE JEW FIRST"

The first year we started Gateway Church, we began to give to Jewish evangelism—*first*. Before we give to any other ministries or missionaries, we give to Jewish evangelism. It's such a priority with me that I told our business pastor, "On the first day of every month, I want you to write a check to such-and-such Jewish ministry. I want you to do it on January 1, February 1, March 1, April 1, throughout the year. Make sure the *very first* check we write each month is not to the electric company or even to pay the staff—the first check we write is for Jewish evangelism."

As a result, God has blessed us tremendously as a church. We paid cash for 14 acres of land when we were 10 months old. We paid cash for our first building. We paid cash for an expansion, and we now own 190 acres next to the freeway, 10 minutes west of Dallas/Fort Worth Airport. God has blessed us with resources, and I believe it's because we're doing it His way—we're giving to the Jewish people first.

We have a rabbi and another Jewish minister on staff, and we place an ad in the newspaper every week for "Ask the Rabbi."

We have a Messianic Jewish service each month, and Jewish people come with newspaper in hand to yell at our rabbi for a while before each service. Just a few months ago, six Jews came to yell at him before a service, and all six accepted *Yeshua* as their Messiah that night—all six!

We're radical about it! Our Jewish service is on the first Friday of every month. We have regular services on Saturdays and Sundays, but *the first service* we have every month is for Jewish people. We've put God's priorities first, and I believe that's the reason God is blessing us. God put it in our hearts a long time ago to take the gospel "to the Jew first" (see Romans 1:16). We are concerned for Jewish people and concerned about God's order, and God has blessed Gateway Church because of it. He has poured tremendous resources into our hands because we are doing it His way.

God is a God of order. God doesn't think His order is the "right way" or the "best way"—He thinks it's the *only way*! And that's what He blesses. If you want to be blessed, do it His way. He has an order for how we are to approach certain things and He wants His order accomplished. In the Old Testament, we read that He had an order for the Tabernacle. He had an order for the Temple. He had an order for preparing and eating food. He had an order for offering sacrifices and prayers and worship. Don't you think God has an order for world evangelism?

Before we go any further, you must understand that God operates in opposites. His plan is always the opposite of our plan. If someone does you wrong, you plan to tell him off. You go through the conversation in your mind, planning exactly what you're going to say to him. According to God, all that planning is time and energy wasted, because His plan—the opposite of yours—is to forgive your offender, act as if it never happened, and bless him. God's law of opposites says that if you want to have authority, you must be under authority. If you want to receive, you must give. If you want to be first, you must be last. If you want to live, you must die to self.

Let's see how the law of opposites applies to evangelism. The deception of the enemy has convinced many people in the Church to think that if they want to reach Muslims (for example) with the gospel, they need to hate Jews, because radical Islam hates Jews. But do you know what God's law of opposites says? If you want to reach Muslims, *love* Jews! I know this is God's plan because it's scriptural—and because it's opposite from the plan I would have come up with! This makes no common sense at all, but God's Word says that the way to love and take the gospel to the world is to love and take the gospel to Jews. Remember Ezekiel 36 and Romans 11:15? As God shows Himself holy through the Jewish people, the nations around Israel will turn to Him.

Many pastors quote Romans 1:16, but they only quote the first part—"For I'm not ashamed of the gospel of Christ, for it is the power of God unto salvation to everyone who believes … "—and stop right there. But that's not where the apostle Paul stopped! He went on to write, "to the Jew first, and also to the Greek."

God will bless any church or any person who will take the gospel into the world, because He wants the whole world saved. The Bible says, "How beautiful are the feet of those who bring good news" (Romans 10:15). That word "beautiful" means "perfect timing," like a spring flower in full bloom. Here's what God is saying: *Those who bring good news will always walk in perfect timing.* When you walk in the Spirit, when you live your life taking the gospel to people, "divine coincidences" happen around you all the time.

God blesses those who take the gospel, that's true. But the full truth of the Word is that God blesses those who take the gospel "to the Jew first, and also to the Greek," that is, Gentiles or non-Jews. It's like tithing: If you give the first portion of your income to the Lord, the rest is blessed. If you give the first portion of your evangelism efforts to Jewish people, the rest is blessed. It's God's order.

Jesus followed God's order during His earthly ministry. He said, "I was not sent except to the lost sheep of the house of Israel" (Matthew 15:24). He took the gospel to the Jews first. In the same way, the apostles were sent out by the Holy Spirit and "preached the word of God in the synagogues of the Jews" (see Acts 13:1-5, 14; 14:1; 17:10).

In Acts 18:5-8, we read that Paul preached to the Jews and became angry when they opposed him and blasphemed. It is a misinterpretation of this incident that has led some in the Church to fall into error, believing that Paul switched his ministry to the Gentiles *alone*. Yes, Paul was angry and, yes, he was called to preach to the Gentiles—but neither his anger nor his calling stopped him from preaching "to the Jew first."

In Acts 18:7-8, we read that Paul moved into the house next door to the synagogue and won the ruler of the synagogue to the Lord. In Acts 18:19 and 19:8, we see that Paul went to the synagogues to preach. Paul knew it was God's order to preach "to the Jew first." God wants the whole earth saved, but His order for world evangelism demands that we begin with the Jewish people. Then the rest of our world evangelism will be blessed.

THE COMING REVIVAL

Is God concerned about the Jewish people? Paul answers this important question in Romans 11:

> I say then, has God cast away His people? Certainly not! For I also am
> an Israelite, of the seed of Abraham, of the tribe of Benjamin (v. 1) ... I
> say then, have they stumbled that they should fall? Certainly not! But
> through their fall to provoke them to jealousy, salvation has come to
> the Gentiles. Now if their fall is riches for the world, and their failure
> riches for the Gentiles, how much more their fullness! (v. 11-12) ... For
> if their being cast away is the reconciling of the world, what will their
> acceptance be but life from the dead? (v. 15).

If the Jews' falling away was salvation and blessing for Gentiles, how much more will their coming back be? Their acceptance will be "life from the dead," which is another way to say "resurrection of the dead." And what do the Scriptures mean when they refer to "the resurrection of the dead"? The second coming of Christ! There is a coming day when Israel will accept their Messiah, before the end comes. Jesus prophesied it in Matthew 23:37-39:

> O Jerusalem, Jerusalem, the one who kills the prophets and stones
> those who are sent to her! How often I wanted to gather your children

together, as a hen gathers her chicks under her wings, but you were not willing! See! Your house is left to you desolate; for I say to you, you shall see Me no more till you say, "Blessed is He who comes in the name of the Lord!"

There is a worldwide revival coming before the end of the world, and let me tell you what sets it off: the Jewish people accepting their Messiah. I love how *THE MESSAGE* captures Paul's excitement and urgency in the Romans 11 passage:

The next question is, "Are they down for the count? Are they out of this for good?" And the answer is a clear-cut no. Ironically when they walked out, they left the door open and the outsiders walked in. But the next thing you know, the Jews were starting to wonder if perhaps they had walked out on a good thing. Now, if their leaving triggered this worldwide coming of non-Jewish outsiders to God's kingdom, just imagine the effect of their coming back! What a homecoming!

But I don't want to go on about them. It's you, the outsiders, that I'm concerned with now. Because my personal assignment is focused on the so-called outsiders, I make as much of this as I can when I'm among my Israelite kin, the so-called insiders, hoping they'll realize what they're missing and want to get in on what God is doing. If their falling out initiated this worldwide coming together, their recovery is going to set off something even better: mass homecoming! If the first thing the Jews did, even though it was wrong for them, turned out for your good, just think what's going to happen when they get it right!

Wow! Isn't it exciting to think about what that day will be like? Can you imagine how much the world will shift? Since the day when my eyes were opened and my heart was burdened to pray for Jerusalem, I have had a prophetic word: One day God will use me to reach Muslims, and the walls of Islam will be broken down just like the Berlin Wall—*in a day*. I believe that the wall that traps Muslims in oppression and deceit will fall, just as Communism's wall of oppression in East Germany fell—*in a day*! That may sound like wishful thinking, but no one believed it could happen in Germany or Poland or Czechoslovakia or the former Soviet Union, either!

Satan knows that for this massive change to occur, the Jewish people have to accept Jesus—so Satan has done everything he can to get the Church to hate Jews. The Jewish people have suffered persecution for hundreds of years—not at the hands of Muslims (that didn't start until 1920), but at the hands of the Church. The Church has burned Jewish houses, raped Jewish women, and murdered Jewish fathers after making them dig their own graves. The Church, with crosses on their chest, tortured Jews and screamed at them, "This is for what you did to our Lord."

Many Jews are more afraid of a cross than a swastika because of the cruel history of persecution from the Church.

In the last generation, however, God has stirred the hearts of believers. We have begun to love Israel and to see that God still has a plan for them. More Jews have accepted Jesus in the last 50 years than in the previous 1,960 or so. Jews are coming to Jesus all over the world. Every month in Gateway's Messianic service, Jews are accepting Christ. That was unheard of only a few decades ago. The revival has begun.

But here's the latest lie of Satan: He's telling the Church that Jewish people don't need to accept Christ—they're going to be saved anyway. Books are being published that promote this lie, and a few popular Bible teachers are teaching it.

I do believe Israel will be saved, but not apart from Jesus. Jesus looked at a Jewish leader named Nicodemus and said, "Most assuredly, I say to you, unless one is born of water and the Spirit, he cannot enter the kingdom of God. That which is born of the flesh is flesh, and that which is born of the Spirit is spirit. Do not marvel that I said to you, 'You must be born again'" (Matthew 3:5-7). Jesus said to the Jewish apostles, "I am the way, the truth, and the life. No one comes to the Father except through Me" (John 14:6).

Jewish people must accept Jesus. Satan says, "You'll offend them." Well, I'd rather temporarily offend them than deliver them to an eternity in hell.

This year Gateway Church gave $3 million to missions. Of that amount, $1 million went to Jewish evangelism and $2 million toward Gentile evangelism. I'm not saying don't evangelize the world! We support Arab-Palestinian churches too. We give in 36 countries all over the world. We're taking the gospel to everyone, but we're taking it to Jewish people first.

This is God's prescribed order. When we give to the Jewish people first, the rest is blessed. I believe that's why God has so blessed us as a church: A long time ago we decided to give "to the Jew first."

THE FATHER'S HOUSE: A PARABLE

After a question-and-answer session at a conference, a pastor approached me and asked, "Why is Gateway so blessed?" and I gave him an answer off the top of my head.

The next morning in my quiet time, the Lord said, "Your answer was wrong!"

"What's the right answer, Lord? Why is Gateway so blessed?" This is what God said to me, in a parable:

> There was an orphanage with a thousand kids in it. The head of the orphanage was a harsh, mean man. All of the kids were treated horribly.
> There was a wealthy, loving father who lived close by, and he decided to adopt 10 of the kids. His plan was to bless those 10 and be

so wonderful to them that the other 990 would all want to be adopted too. And that's just what happened. Many (not all) of the 990 kids saw how wonderful life could be with a loving father, and some of them started walking out and going to the father's house.

But then a very sad thing happened: When so many of the remaining 990 kids started coming into the father's house, the original 10 got jealous and left.

And then something even sadder happened: Some of the newly adopted kids started persecuting the 10 who had left, throwing rocks at them and calling them names—driving them further and further away from home.

Then the Lord said to me, "And then one day, Robert, you came to Me with tears in your eyes and said, 'Dad, I have a burden for your original 10 kids that left, and if it's all right with You, I want to try to get them to come back home.' And that's when I reached in my pocket, pulled out my wallet, and said 'How much do you need?'"

That's why Gateway Church is so blessed. We're blessed because we're taking the gospel to the whole world, but we're doing it God's way: "to the Jew first."

Here's my question to you: How do you feel about God's kids who aren't living at home anymore? What is the Holy Spirit speaking to your heart about what you've just read? He might answer you tomorrow in your quiet time, or maybe give you a more complete answer a month from now, but I think He wants to turn you toward His path right now.

God has a plan for you and He wants you to live "the blessed life." Now that you understand God's order, the principles presented in the previous chapters will give you the tools to do so.

APPENDIX: STUDY GUIDE

CHAPTER 1
THE UNEXPECTED ADVENTURE

Key Scripture

Deuteronomy 28:1-14

Points to Ponder

- Being blessed means having supernatural power working for you.
- The days of the blessed person are filled with divine coincidences and heavenly meaning.

Food for Thought

1. In this chapter, I relate an incident in which God revealed to a woman behind a gas station cash register that I was an evangelist and that she was to pay for my gas. The "idea that the Spirit of God would speak to someone and instruct them to give" (p. 11) has become a centerpiece of my ministry and Christian walk. On a scale of 1 to 10, how would you rate your ability to hear God?

2. In story after story, I relate the joy of giving vehicles, special missionary offerings, and other gifts. What is the most joy you have ever experienced from making a gift?

3. Describe the difference between the following experiences. In which cases should you give?

   - God tells you to give.
   - Your pastor or a well-meaning volunteer asks you to give to your church or another worthy cause.
   - A Christian friend or relative asks for money for a personal emergency.
   - A non-Christian friend or relative asks for money for a personal emergency.

CHAPTER 2
GOD MUST BE FIRST

Key Scripture

Exodus 13:12–13

Points to Ponder

- Money is a test from God.

- Tithing means giving to God before you see if you're going to have enough.

- Am I robbing God?

Food for Thought

1. In our culture we have a saying: Time is money. Do you agree that the firstfruits principle should be applied to both our time and our money? Give an example of how applying that principle would change how you use your time and money.

2. This chapter shares that the principle of giving the firstfruits means "giving to God before you see if you're going to have enough" (p. 22). How comfortable are you with this type of giving?

3. Proverbs 3:9 commands us to "honor the Lord with [our] possessions." I teach that the primary way we use our possessions to honor God is through our gifts of tithes and offerings. In what other ways can we use our possessions to honor God?

4. Satan uses fear to keep us from being financially faithful. What can you do when Satan attacks you with fear about tithing? What Scripture can you memorize and bring to mind? What song of blessing and praise could you sing? Is there an accountability partner you can call to pray for you?

CHAPTER 3
LIFE, NOT LAW

Key Scripture

Matthew 6

Points to Ponder

- We need to acknowledge that we are stewards, not owners.

- Tithing blesses God; and in return, He blesses the one who tithes, creating an upward cycle of blessing and abundance.

- True tithing comes from the heart—not from a legalistic mind.

- Tithing is not law—it is life.

- The devourer is rebuked!

- The righteousness of grace always exceeds the righteousness of the law.

Food for Thought

1. From the Sermon on the Mount, we see that Jesus uses the Old Testament law to set a higher standard. Instead of "Thou shalt not kill" (Matthew 5:21, KJV), Jesus tells us to not even be angry with someone (see v. 22). How does this principle apply to the tithe?

2. In Genesis 28, God speaks to Jacob in a dream and details how He plans to bless him. Jacob's response is to worship God and vow to give Him a tenth of all he is given. Make a list of the ways God has blessed you. Take time to worship and thank Him for what He has done and is going to do in your life. How do thankfulness and worship help prepare our hearts for giving?

3. In 1 Corinthians 13:3, Paul says that even if we give everything we own to the poor but have no love, it profits us nothing. How does this verse relate to my teaching about the importance of the heart to tithing?

4. Have you ever been part of a fund-raising effort that not only reached its goal but also went over it? What psychological effect did that success and abundance have on the members of the organization? Imagine how your pastor would feel if the offering this Sunday were well above the weekly budget. What impact would it have on his attitude as a minister in the following week?

CHAPTER 4
THE PRINCIPLE OF MULTIPLICATION

Key Scripture

Luke 9:12–17

Points to Ponder

- Something must be blessed before it can multiply.

- Only what is given away can multiply.

Food for Thought

1. Do you agree that worry is our way of trying to figure out in advance how God is going to provide for us? Is God always absent from the equation when you worry?

2. In Luke 9:12–17, there was not only enough to feed the multitude, but there was also a lot left over. Read Ephesians 3:14–21. How does this passage apply to a mind-set of abundance. What can you do to help yourself maintain a mind-set of abundance throughout the day?

3. In the story of the widow's mites (Luke 21:1–4), Jesus suggests that even though the widow put in only two mites, she gave more than all the wealthy people who went before her. How does this story expand your understanding of the principle of multiplication? Is it possible that small gifts from people who are giving a greater proportion of their income benefit the person and the Church more than large gifts from wealthy people who are giving proportionately less?

CHAPTER 5
BREAKING THE SPIRIT OF MAMMON

Key Scriptures

Deuteronomy 8:18; Matthew 6:24

Points to Ponder

- The spirit of mammon says, "You don't need God. Trust in riches."

- Greed, covetousness, and selfishness are all manifestations of the spirit of mammon.

- Spirit-led giving simultaneously diminishes Satan's kingdom and makes us more like our heavenly Father.

- Giving is not a get-rich-quick scheme; it is a lay-down-your-life challenge.

- The spirit of pride says, "Wealth comes from hard work." The spirit of poverty says, "Wealth comes from the devil."

Food for Thought

1. Mammon tells us that money is the answer to every problem. We often talk about "throwing money" at a problem to indicate that money can be the easy solution but not always the best solution. Can you think of examples when making more money available has led to disappointing results?

2. What aspects of money make you afraid? Does thinking about retirement make you anxious? Do you avoid balancing your checkbook? What behaviors do you have that show you are afraid of money?

3. I say that being a giver will result in blessings. Would you continue to give tithes and offerings even if your only reward was salvation through Jesus Christ? Read Hebrews 11:13 and consider how it might apply.

4. In this chapter, I give several warning signs that we are looking to men rather than God as our source of provision. Share your reaction in the following situations:

   - It's been a tough month financially, and to top it off, your car needs an unbudgeted repair.

- You've worked hard for the last six months expecting a bonus from your employer. A downturn in the economy makes it impossible for your employer to give you the bonus.

- You have been generous with your church, and you have also saved carefully for your retirement by buying stock in your company. You learn from the newspaper that mismanagement of the retirement fund has resulted in it losing more than half its value.

- When these kinds of financial setbacks occur, how can we look to God rather than men for provision?

CHAPTER 6
IT TAKES A HEART TRANSPLANT

Key Scriptures

Deuteronomy 5:29; Deuteronomy 15:15; Proverbs 16:2; Luke 6:38; James 4:3

Points to Ponder

- You always receive back more than you give.

- God doesn't want us to catch the vision of getting. He wants us to catch the vision of giving.

- Practically everyone is a cheerful getter. God wants us to be cheerful givers.

- A properly focused heart is more excited about the giving part than the receiving part.

- Selfishness can attack us before we give, but grief can attack us after we give.

- When we're grateful, we're generous.

- Our attitudes toward possessions have a powerful ability to expose the true nature of our hearts.

Food for Thought

1. I think the key to having right motives is to renew our minds and to understand that selfish thoughts are more than just unkind; they are wicked (see Deuteronomy 15:9). Is an unselfish attitude an act of the will, a matter of practice, a spiritual discipline, or a work of grace in one's life?

2. Develop three strategies you can do in advance of making a gift or offering to prevent giver's remorse.

3. Think about a time when you lost some money. Maybe it was in the stock market, maybe it was in a misplaced wallet, or maybe you made a bad purchase. What did that experience tell you about the importance of money in your life?

4. How does 1 Timothy 6:5 (Paul's condemnation of people who see godliness as a means of financial gain) apply to our study of motives and giving?

CHAPTER 7
DO THE RIGHT THING

Key Scripture

Matthew 6:21

Points to Ponder

- Get out of debt.

- Never manipulate others.

- Give.

- God always honors doing the right thing.

- If you're going to live the lifestyle of a giver, you're going to have to make the lifestyle adjustments that allow you to give.

- IO stands for Instant Obedience.

Food for Thought

1. Read Deuteronomy 15:6 and 28:12. In both passages, God reveals His will that the people of Israel be lenders, not borrowers. Some believers think it is always wrong to borrow money, even for a mortgage. What, in your view, is the balanced biblical position?

2. In marriage counseling, couples are sometimes advised to act like they love one another, trusting that eventually feelings of love will follow. Do you believe that if you begin to put your treasure in godly activities (the local church), your heart will follow? What will you do this week to be financially obedient?

3. Can you give an example of a time when God tested your obedience? What was the outcome?

CHAPTER 8
THE GIFT OF GIVING

Key Scripture

Romans 12:6-8

Points to Ponder

- God has given the gift of giving to individuals in the Church who have a desire to give large amounts if the vision is large and worthy.

- People who have the gift of giving can sense manipulation from a mile away.

- People who have the gift of giving give by the voice of the Spirit.

- Wealth can be a blessing from God and a product of things such as diligence and generosity.

- People who have the gift of giving are very frugal but also very generous.

- When you're around someone who has the gift of giving, talk about anything but money.

- People who have the gift of giving don't want to be a band-aid. They want to be a cure.

Food for Thought

1. I teach that people who have the gift of giving should beware of people who are ungrateful, insensitive, and manipulative. Does that sound like anyone you know? How should we respond when people take advantage of us?

2. Do you think the passage in Romans about the gift of giving is specifically about financial giving, or is it broader than that?

3. Have you asked God to give you the gift of giving? Is that a gift you want your children to have?

4. I believe wealthy individuals often don't feel welcome in churches. Can you give an example of how wealth (or lack of it) has made it difficult to have a relationship with someone?

CHAPTER 9
GOD REWARDS GOOD STEWARDSHIP

Key Scriptures

1 Corinthians 3:8; Hebrews 11:6

Points to Ponder

- God is a rewarder.

- Our belief determines where we will spend eternity, and our behavior determines how we will spend eternity.

- We will never see God's miraculous power given to poor stewards!

- "Do [kingdom] business till I come" (Luke 19:13).

- Poor stewards lose resources. Good stewards receive more.

- Every day God sees the purchases we make and the money we give.

- We can't help others if we don't care for what God has given us.

Food for Thought

1. According to the parable of the talents, God has "delivered His goods to us" (p. 105). He has given us natural abilities and spiritual gifts that we are to use for the kingdom. Make a list of the natural abilities and spiritual gifts God has given you. Are you using them for the kingdom? If not, what are the obstacles?

2. Do you agree that poor stewardship can keep us from being effective in the kingdom? We know that God uses imperfect people to advance His purposes, but can you think of an example from the Old or New Testament in which God elevated a person who was financially irresponsible?

3. In talking about the consequences of poor stewardship, I give the example of the couple who decided to buy a new barbeque grill for $300 when they had many household bills to pay. If instead of purchasing the barbeque grill, they felt led to make a $300 gift to the church and they came to you for advice, what would you say? Is it possible to be irresponsible in our giving?

CHAPTER 10
NEED, GREED, OR SEED

Key Scripture

2 Corinthians 9:6–11

Points to Ponder

- It all comes down to the heart.

- God is able.

- All grace, abundance, and sufficiency are a direct result of sowing bountifully from a cheerful heart.

- It is at the level of sufficiency and abundance that we're all tested.

- Financial growth is a by-product of bountiful sowing.

- You reap after you sow.

- You have to start where you are.

Food for Thought

1. What specific behaviors are associated with purposing in your heart what you should give?

2. I believe that the only way to give cheerfully is if God does a work in your heart. What can you do to make it possible for God to do a work in your heart?

3. 2 Corinthians 9:10–11 suggests a relationship between sowing seed and bearing the fruit of righteousness. Do you believe our ability to exhibit the fruit of the Spirit is tied to our stewardship? Explain your thinking.

4. What is the test of need? What is the test of greed? What is the test of seed?

CHAPTER 11
GOD REWARDS GENEROSITY

Key Scripture

John 12:1-8

Points to Ponder

- Wherever you find generosity, you will find selfishness battling for control.

- A selfish person will always find good reasons not to be generous.

- Selfishness always looks after self by pointing at someone else.

- We will frequently be tempted in the area of our greatest weakness.

- God wants to help us turn our area of greatest potential defeat into our area of greatest victory.

- True riches are souls.

- Generosity is extravagant.

- It's not the amount; it's the heart.

- God has a purpose for every gift.

Food for Thought

1. Ask yourself the fundamental questions that I pose in this chapter: Are you selfish or are you generous? Which one has the upper hand in your life?

2. Jesus put Judas in charge of the offering box, Judas's area of weakness. Can you think of a comparable situation in your life? Think of the areas over which you have responsibility. Are any of them areas of weakness?

3. Define these three levels of giving:

   - Tithes

   - Offerings

   - Extravagant offerings

4. If you can, give an example from your life, or from the life of someone you know, of a gift to the church that fulfilled a specific need unknown to the giver.

CHAPTER 12
GUARANTEED FINANCIAL RESULTS

Key Scripture

John 2:5

Points to Ponder

- When you touch God, He immediately touches you back.
- The trap the enemy wants us to fall into is worshipping the blessings rather than the Blessor.
- We were all born takers; we are born-again givers.
- As soon as you hear God say it—do it.
- When we give just to give, the results are guaranteed.

Food for Thought

1. Why is God searching for hearts that are completely His?
2. How can you keep from seeking after the blessings that come from God's hand rather than seeking God's face?
3. What do you identify as the key to guaranteed financial results?

ENDNOTES

Chapter 2: God Must Be First

1. Mike Hayes (lecture, the Zion Conference, Trinity Fellowship Church, Amarillo, Texas, January 2000).

Chapter 3: Life, Not Law

1. *The New Unger's Bible Dictionary* (Chicago, IL: Moody Press, 1988), s.v. "tenth."

2. *International Standard Bible Encyclopaedia* (Biblesoft, 1996), CD-ROM.

3. *The New Unger's Bible Dictionary* (Chicago, IL: Moody Press, 1988), s.v. "holy."

Chapter 5: Breaking the Spirit of Mammon

1. *International Standard Bible Encyclopaedia* (Biblesoft, 1996), CD-ROM.

2. Jimmy Evans, telephone conversation with author.

3. *International Standard Bible Encyclopaedia* (Biblesoft, 1996), CD-ROM.

4. Ibid.

Chapter 8: The Gift of Giving

1. Source unknown.

The **Blessed** Life
A GATEWAY DEVOTIONAL

The Blessed Life: A Gateway Devotional
Copyright © 2015 by Gateway Create Publishing
All rights reserved.

Taken from *The Blessed Life* by Robert Morris

Editorial Director *Stacy Burnett*
Senior Editor *Daniel Hopkins*
Editor *Shea Tellefsen*
Copy Editor *Georgette Shuler*
Assistant Editors *Sydnie Shreffler, Katie Smith*
Art Director *Shane Dennehey*
Design *Emanuel Puscas*
Production Design *Katrina Sirmon*
Photographer *Cory Hale*

Requests for information should be addressed to:
Gateway Create Publishing, 810 Mustang Dr, Ste 300, Grapevine, TX 76051

CONTENTS

PREFACE

Living the blessed life has truly been an adventure for Debbie and me. From the beginning of this journey, God has asked us to give in ways that required instant obedience and trust in Him. We've given away multiple vehicles, our retirement savings, and even our home. As a result, God has blessed us more than we could've ever imagined, and He wants to bless you too. It all starts with understanding and applying the principles in this devotional. But first, I want to tell you the story of how it all got started for us.

Long before we started Gateway Church in my living room, I was a traveling evangelist, and all of my income came from love offerings I received from churches when I preached. It could be $800 one week and $200 the next, so it required us to trust God for our finances. There was a month during which I was only scheduled to preach at one church, so this presented a potential budget challenge for us. After I preached, the pastor brought me an envelope and told me it was the largest love offering his little church had ever given. I looked at the check and it was *exactly* what we needed for our monthly budget. I was so relieved and grateful, but then God spoke to me about a missionary who had given a brief update to the congregation earlier that night. The Lord said, "I want you to give him your offering—all of it." I began to panic, and I tried to rationalize and bargain with the Lord, but I knew I had to obey. So I signed over the check to the missionary and as I handed it to him, I asked him not to tell anyone about it.

An hour later, Debbie and I were at a pizza place with some of the church members. I found myself seated across from a well-dressed man I barely knew. He leaned across the table and asked, "How much was your offering tonight?" I was a little flustered by the question, especially because he was a near stranger. I told him the amount, hoping that would be the end of it, but he responded with another question: "Where is the check?" I couldn't believe his nerve! I'm not proud to tell you this, but I lied right through my teeth. I told him my wife had it. "Go get it. I want to see it." I got up and pretended to get it from her. When I returned, I lied again: "She left it in the car." He leaned across the table, got uncomfortably close, and said, "The check's not in the car, Robert." I responded, "How do you know that?" "Because God told me," he said. "And He told me something else."

I will never forget what he said next: "God is about to teach you about giving so that you can teach the body of Christ." With that, he slid a check across the table.

The amount was exactly 10 times what I had given away only an hour earlier. That night was the beginning of this incredible adventure.

Whether you're just starting your blessed life journey or you've been practicing biblical principles on giving for years, when you apply these truths, God will cause you to prosper. More importantly, He will do an amazing work in your heart. It's my hope that this devotional encourages you and helps you discover a life of generosity and abundance that so few ever dare to live.

Pastor Robert Morris

SACRIFICED
OR REDEEMED

"Consecrate to Me all the firstborn, whatever opens the womb among the children of Israel, both of man and beast; it is Mine." Exodus 13:2

When Debbie and I got married, our combined gross income was $600 a month. That's an annual income of $7,200, which was nearly impossible to live on even back then. During that first year, the Lord spoke to us about tithing, so we began to diligently give Him the first tenth of everything that came in. A few months after we started to give our tithe, Debbie got a job that paid $18,000 annually, and I began preaching at revivals, which brought my first year's salary up to $32,000. Our annual income went from $7,200 to $50,000. The next year, my income went up to $72,000, and Debbie was able to quit her job and stay at home. That's a tenfold increase from what we were bringing in during our first year. We continued to tithe and give extravagantly to the Lord and the next year, my income increased to more than $100,000. By God's grace, we were giving more than 70 percent of it away (and having the time of our lives doing it!).

I don't tell this story because I want you to know how much money I make; I tell it because it's an example of what happens when you begin tithing. Most Christians have heard the word "tithe" and most probably know it means to give 10 percent of your increase to the church. However, most Christians don't give their tithe (statistics show churchgoers in America only give 1.7 percent of their income to the kingdom of God), and I think the reason is many Christians don't understand the purpose of tithing or have a distorted view of it. So the very first thing I'm going to do is explain what it actually means to tithe.

Understanding tithing starts with understanding the principle of the firstborn. According to Old Testament law in Exodus 13:2, the firstborn had to be either sacrificed or redeemed because it belonged to God. There was no third option. Every time one of your livestock animals delivered its firstborn, you had to sacrifice it. Or if it was designated unclean, you had to redeem it by sacrificing a clean, spotless lamb in its place. Simply put, the clean firstborn had to be sacrificed and the unclean firstborn had to be redeemed.

With that in mind, think about the story in the New Testament in which John the Baptist meets Jesus on the banks of the Jordan River: John was baptizing one day and looked up to see Jesus walking toward him. At that point, John cried out, "Behold! The Lamb of God who takes away the sin of the world!" (John 1:29)

John perfectly defined the role Jesus came to fill. Jesus was God's firstborn. He was clean—perfect and unblemished in every way. On the other hand, every one of us was born unclean. We were all born sinners with a fully active sin nature. Now, think back to the principle of the firstborn in Exodus. Remember, the law stated if the firstborn animal was clean, it was to be sacrificed. But if the firstborn was unclean, it was to be redeemed with a clean animal. Do you see the symbolic parallel? Jesus Christ was God's firstborn Son. Essentially, Jesus was God's *tithe*.

We find the principle of the firstborn all throughout God's Word. Whether we give Him the first of our time or our finances, tithing is really about giving our first to God. It's not about giving God what's left over after you've paid your bills. It always requires faith to give the first, which is why so few Christians experience the blessings of tithing. By tithing, you're saying, "God, I recognize You first. I'm putting You first in my life, and I trust You to take care of the rest of the things in my life." That's why tithing is so important. It's the primary way we acknowledge that God is first.

....

Prayer
God, thank You for giving Your firstborn Son for me. Thank You for Your sacrifice so I could be redeemed. I want to put You first in all areas of my life. Today, I set aside all the things that may be taking a priority over You in my life. In Jesus' name, Amen.

For Further Study
Exodus 13, 34:19–20; Romans 5:8, 8:29; Matthew 16:25

FIRST OF
THE FIRST

"The first of the firstfruits of your land you shall bring into the house of the Lord your God." Exodus 23:19

I magine I've given you 10 one-dollar bills and you have them laid out side by side. My first question is, "How much is the tithe on this money?" I think most Christians would get this one right. The tithe on *10* dollars is, obviously, *one* dollar. But here's the more difficult question. Which *one* is the firstfruit? Is it the one on your left or is it the one on your right? Let me answer that for you. The firstfruit is the first one spent or given. In other words, when you get paid, the first check you write should be the tithe check. I first heard this illustration from Pastor Mike Hayes of Covenant Church, and I like it because it perfectly represents what the Bible says about firstfruits.

The Word makes it clear that we need to honor the Lord with the firstfruits of our increase. When we do, according to Proverbs 3:10, it honors the Lord and our "barns will be filled with plenty, and [our] vats will overflow." Notice today's Scripture designates "the house of the Lord" as the proper place to give our firstfruits. It doesn't say to give them to a television ministry or missionary, although I believe in supporting missionary work and worthy media ministries.

Another example of firstfruits in Scripture can be found in the book of Joshua. After Jericho fell, the Lord gave the Israelites strict instructions not to keep any of the spoils. All of it belonged to Him. Why did the Lord say that all of the silver and gold from Jericho had to be given to the Lord's house? Because it was the *first* city conquered in the Promised Land. It was the firstfruit.

God didn't say, "Conquer 10 cities and give Me all the spoils from the tenth one." He essentially said, "Give Me the first and you can have the rest." That took faith, of course—and so does tithing. One Israelite disregarded God's clear instructions. Joshua 7:1 says a man named Achan took some for himself and became "accursed." Think about that. When the spoils were given to God, they were "consecrated" or set apart for God's house. But when a man took some for himself, it was actually cursing Israel's efforts to take the Promised Land. Consecrated or cursed—that's exactly what the tithe is all through the Bible. If we take the firstfruits for ourselves, it becomes a curse because we've stolen from God.

Is it really an act of faith to give 10 percent after all your other bills are paid? What does it say about our priorities when we willingly pay everybody else first and then see if there is enough left to give God His portion? The first portion we spend should be the tithe. That is the firstfruit. And according to Exodus 13, the first portion is the redemptive portion. That's why it's so important that our tithe is our firstfruit. The first portion has the power to redeem the rest, and I promise you a redeemed 90 percent can go a lot further than a cursed 100 percent.

Prayer

Lord, give me the faith to give You the first of my finances. I want the money you've put in my possession to be consecrated for Your house—not cursed. In Jesus' name, Amen.

For Further Study

Exodus 22:29–31; Joshua 6:18–19; Joshua 7; Malachi 3:8–12

MORE THAN MONEY

"For if the firstfruit is holy, the lump is also holy; and if the root is holy, so are the branches." Romans 11:16

When you think of the word "tithe," what's the first thing that comes to your mind? Most people probably think of money, but it actually has little to do with money. For God, tithing is an issue of the heart. Genesis 4:3–5 tells the story of Cain and Abel bringing their offerings to the Lord, and it gives us a lot of insight into what God is looking at when we give: "And in the process of time it came to pass that Cain brought an offering of the fruit of the ground to the Lord. Abel also brought of the firstborn of his flock and of their fat. And the Lord respected Abel and his offering, but He did not respect Cain and his offering. And Cain was very angry, and his countenance fell."

People have wondered for years why God respected Abel's offering and not Cain's. The Word makes it clear the offering Abel brought was the firstborn of his flock, but it doesn't say Cain brought the firstfruits of his crops. In fact, it says, "and in the process of time." In other words, Cain grew his crops and then, "in the process of time," got around to bringing an offering to the Lord. The implication is that he didn't bring his firstfruits to the Lord. Could that be why God did not respect Cain's offering? I believe so. Abel, on the other hand, brought the firstborn of his flock to the Lord, and God accepted his offering.

Here's the lesson for us: God is looking at our hearts when we give. And when we give the first of our firstfruits, or our tithe, God receives and respects that offering because it takes a lot of faith to give to God before we pay our mortgage, our car payment, or the IRS.

There was much more at stake than money when Abraham offered his firstborn son, Isaac, to the Lord (Genesis 22). Abraham didn't wait to see if he had 10 sons before he gave his first one. Nor did God go to Abraham when he only had Isaac and say, "After you have four or five more sons, I'm going to come to you and ask you for one of them." No, God asked for the first when *one* was all he had! Abraham only had the *promise* of having more sons. It took faith for Abraham to offer Isaac. And faith is precisely what tithing requires. It's giving God the first, in faith. Many people *say* they're putting God first, but true tithing is where the rubber meets the road. It's where we walk what we talk. It's also one of the ways God blesses and protects us.

When Satan comes against you with fear and says, "You're going to go broke, your marriage is going to fail, you're going to get a disease," you can firmly reply, "No, I'm a tither, and because I tithe, the Bible says that God will rebuke the devourer *for my sake*. Yes, for *my* sake! God is first in my life, and God is going to redeem and protect everything else in my life!" Putting God first in our lives is what tithing is all about. It's not about money; it's about revealing the state of our hearts.

<hr>

Prayer

God, thank You for blessing me with everything I have. Help me to understand Your heart for tithing, and give me the faith to give You the first of my increase. In Jesus' name, Amen.

For Further Study

Genesis 22; Leviticus 27:30; 1 Corinthians 16:1–2

LIFE,
NOT LAW

"Then the Lord God took the man and put him in the garden of Eden to tend and keep it. And the Lord God commanded the man, saying, 'Of every tree of the garden you may freely eat; but of the tree of the knowledge of good and evil you shall not eat, for in the day that you eat of it you shall surely die.'" Genesis 2:15–17

Over the years, many well-meaning but misguided Christians have reacted to my message about tithing by telling me they don't tithe because "tithing is part of 'the law.'" With all my heart, I want you to understand something: Tithing is not law—*it is life!* Let me say that in a different way. I don't tithe because it was a part of the Old Testament law; I tithe because it's life to me and my family. In fact, tithing isn't just limited to the Old Testament—it's a principle that runs throughout the Word of God, predating the law of Moses by thousands of years.

Tithing (firstfruits or firstborn) was in operation in Genesis as Abraham was asked to offer Isaac and when he gave a tenth of the spoils from Sodom and Gomorrah to Melchizedek—a representation of Jesus Christ (Hebrews 5–7). This principle goes back even further. In today's verse, we see the principle of the tithe in God's instructions to Adam and Eve about the trees in the Garden of Eden.

Notice that in giving Adam and Eve stewardship of the garden, God gave them every tree to eat freely from except for one. Exercising faithful stewardship of the garden meant leaving that one tree alone. They were not to take that fruit for themselves and consume it. Being faithful stewards meant *life* to Adam and Eve. By choosing to eat the fruit of that tree, they were acting like *owners* rather than *stewards*.

Isn't that precisely how the principle of the tithe operates for us today? God gives us stewardship responsibility over our lives. Though it *all* belongs to Him, He richly gives us all things to enjoy (1 Timothy 6:17). But He has asked us not to touch the firstfruits because they're His. We demonstrate faithful stewardship and show God that we realize we are stewards, not owners, when we give Him the tithe.

You can see from these examples that the tithe completely transcends Old Testament law. But that shouldn't surprise us, because so do many other eternal principles.

Imagine what you would think if one evening you invited me over to your house for dinner and as I was walking out the door after a great meal, I grabbed your television and took it home. What if when you asked, "Why did you do that? The Bible says you're not supposed to steal," my response was, "Well, 'Thou shalt not steal' was part of the law. I'm not under the law. I'm under grace."

I'm using an absurd illustration to make an important point. Just because something was mentioned in the law of Moses doesn't mean we can throw it out now. Let me address this issue in another way. If something was *wrong* under the law, can it be *right* under grace? In other words, since stealing was wrong under the law, is it now right under grace? Of course not!

Now let me turn the question around. If something was *right* under the law, can it be *wrong* under grace? Specifically, tithing was clearly the right thing to do under the law, but is it now the wrong thing to do under grace? Certainly not.

Once you see tithing as life instead of a law originating in the Old Testament, your heart will change and tithing will become a blessing instead of a burden.

Prayer
Lord, thank You that You never change. Help me to embrace tithing as a blessing instead of a law I have to follow, and show me how to be a good steward. In Jesus' name, Amen.

For Further Study
Genesis 14:18–20; Hebrews 5–7; 1 Timothy 6:17; Romans 6:15

05

UNDER
GRACE

*"Do not think that I came to destroy the law or the Prophets.
I did not come to destroy but to fulfill." Matthew 5:17*

There are a lot of excuses I hear people make about why they don't tithe, and some of them are rather humorous. My favorite excuse, and it's the one I hear most often, is, "I'm under grace, not the law." People think that because Jesus fulfilled the Old Testament law, they're off the hook when it comes to tithing. We touched on this yesterday, but I want to show you why this can't be true by explaining what the law of grace *actually* is and how it works.

The grace of God really is amazing. Here's the key phrase I want you to remember: The righteousness of grace always exceeds the righteousness of the law. This is the essence of what Jesus said in Matthew 5:17–20:

> Do not think that I came to destroy the law or the Prophets. I did not come to destroy but to fulfill. For assuredly, I say to you, till heaven and earth pass away, one jot or one tittle will by no means pass from the law till all is fulfilled. Whoever therefore breaks one of the least of these commandments, and teaches men so, shall be called least in the kingdom of heaven; but whoever does and teaches them, he shall be called great in the kingdom of heaven. For I say to you, that *unless your righteousness exceeds the righteousness of the scribes and Pharisees, you will by no means enter the kingdom of heaven* (emphasis added).

Let me reiterate the key phrase I want you to remember—the righteousness of grace *always* exceeds the righteousness of the law. Notice that each time Jesus points to an Old Covenant law, He then sets a higher standard under New Covenant grace. This doesn't just go for the rule of tithing but for every aspect of the law.

Here's an example: In Exodus 20:13 and Deuteronomy 5:17, the law said not to commit murder, but in Matthew 5:22, Jesus said don't even be angry with your brother. It's a higher standard! In Exodus 20:14 and Deuteronomy 5:18, the law said not to commit adultery, but in Matthew 5:28 Jesus said you shouldn't even look at a woman lustfully. Once again, we see that Jesus is setting a higher standard. In other words, the righteousness that grace demands (and Jesus *is* grace) goes further than that which the law demands.

That's why I smile when someone says to me, "I don't tithe because I'm not under the law. I'm under grace." I almost always respond by saying, "Oh, so you give according to grace?" "Yes, that's right." Then I say, "Great! That means you give much more than 10 percent, because the righteousness of grace always exceeds the righteousness of the law. It's a higher standard."

When we give according to grace, we'll give more than the tithe. Under grace, tithing is simply the starting point for giving. And when you start understanding that the law of grace always exceeds the Old Covenant law, your life will totally change.

Prayer
Lord, thank You that Your grace brings freedom. Instead of being burdened by the law, help me to live by the higher standards that grace sets. In Jesus' name, Amen.

For Further Study
Exodus 20:13-14, Deuteronomy 5:17-18, Matthew 5:22, 28

06

PASSING
THE TEST

"For where your treasure is, there your heart will be also."
Matthew 6:21

T oday's Scripture is a very familiar passage, but I want you to notice how it's worded. It doesn't say, "Where your heart is, there your treasure will be also" (even though many people quote and apply it that way). It says that your heart follows your treasure. That is why tithing represents a test for every Christian. When translated from the Bible, *tithe* literally means "tenth" or "a tenth part."

Do you know what the number 10 represents all through the Bible? *Testing*. Let me give you a few examples. How many plagues were there in Egypt? In other words, how many times did God test Pharaoh's heart? The answer is 10. How many commandments are there? Or another way to say it is, in how many ways is our obedience tested? The answer is 10. How many times did God test Israel while they were wandering in the wilderness? And how many times did God test Jacob's heart (by allowing his wages to be changed) when he was working for Laban? Or how many days was Daniel tested in the first chapter of the book of Daniel? In each case, the answer is, of course, 10.

The pattern continues in the New Testament. In Matthew 25, 10 virgins had their preparedness tested. Ten days of testing are mentioned in Revelation 2:10. We can see from these examples in the Word (and many more like them) that 10 is associated with testing. And the tithe represents the ultimate "heart test" for the believer.

The test is how we handle our money. The outcome of that test determines whether He can trust us with true riches or not. That's why, for us as Christians, money is more than just a means for buying things. Jesus spent 30 percent of His time teaching on money for a reason. As today's verse shows us, God knows where our heart is by where our treasure is. If you say, "My heart is in the kingdom of God," your bank account will either validate or refute that claim.

And what's interesting about this test is that it's the only area in which God has invited *us* to test *Him*: "'Bring the whole tithe into the storehouse, that there may be food in my house. *Test me in this*,' says the Lord Almighty, 'and see if I will not throw open the floodgates of heaven and pour out so much blessing that you will not have room enough for it'" (Malachi 3:10, NIV, emphasis added).

The truth of this passage seems so simple to me. If I tithe, I'm blessed; if I don't, I'm cursed. *Hmmm, that's a tough decision. Let me think about that. Tithe—I'm blessed. Don't tithe—I'm cursed. Blessings? Or curses?* For me, this one really isn't that hard to figure out.

Still unsure about this tithing business? Then take God up on the offer He makes in Malachi 3:10. Test Him on it! God is essentially saying, "Test Me in this, I dare you, I double-dog dare you!" (Excuse my East Texas paraphrasing.) But clearly, God is saying, "Test Me." That's why I want to extend a friendly challenge to you. Do the test! Begin to honor the Lord diligently with your firstfruits—the tithe—and see what happens.

....

Prayer

Lord, I place my treasure, and therefore my heart, with You. I want You to be first in my life. I pray that You would bless my finances as I set apart Your tithe. In Jesus' name, Amen.

For Further Study

Exodus 7-11, 20:1-17; Luke 16:11; Song of Solomon 1:6

BLESSINGS AND BENEFITS

"Since the people began to bring the offerings into the house of the Lord, we have had enough to eat and have plenty left, for the Lord has blessed His people; and what is left is this great abundance." 2 Chronicles 31:10

Can you imagine what the body of Christ could accomplish if every believer tithed? I ask this because based on a statistic we learned a few days ago, American Christians only give 1.7 percent of their income to the church. Keep that in mind as we look at 1 Corinthians 16:1-2: "Now concerning the collection for the saints, as I have given orders to the churches of Galatia, so you must do also: On the first day of the week let each one of you lay something aside, storing up as he may prosper, that there be no collections when I come."

Here, Paul is instructing the Corinthian church to give in accordance to the size of their income so they won't need to take up a special offering when he comes. I long to see the day when we don't have to have candy sales in the foyers of our churches or Saturday car washes, because every member of the church is tithing. However, as long as the Church only gives 1.7 percent of its income, there will be cookies for sale in the lobby. Think about what God's people could accomplish on earth if we faithfully gave Him the first 10 percent so the remaining 90 percent could be redeemed and blessed!

Tithing not only brings provision to the church—*it blesses the giver!*

We see in 2 Chronicles 31:4-10 the story of King Hezekiah ordering the people of Jerusalem to tithe. When the people brought in their firstfruits, Hezekiah was amazed by the "heaps" of grain, wine, oil, honey, oxen, and sheep. He basically said, "Explain this to me; are the people doing okay? They have given so much!" And the priests essentially said, "You need to understand something, King. Since the people began to tithe, God has blessed them. What you see here is the tithe of the abundance with which God has blessed them."

Remember what God said in Malachi 3:10: "Bring all the tithes into the store-house, that there may be food in My house." When Hezekiah commanded the people to do this, they were immediately blessed.

If you aren't already convinced that this Old Testament principle still applies to us today, let's look at the New Testament. In Matthew 23:23, Jesus is admonishing the Pharisees when He says, "Woe to you, scribes and Pharisees, hypocrites! For you pay tithe of mint and anise and cummin, and have neglected the weightier matters of the law: justice and mercy and faith. These you ought to have done, without leaving the others undone."

Jesus is obviously scolding the Pharisees here, but I believe He's doing something much bigger. In my opinion, this is one of the most amazing Scriptures on tithing because Jesus Himself affirmed the tithe. To me, it proves that, when we give our tithe today, we'll receive the same blessing that Hezekiah's people received.

Tithing isn't a grim duty or a dry religious practice. It's an opportunity that blesses the church and brings tremendous benefits to the tither. Imagine the impact the Church would have on the world if every believer tithed.

Prayer

Lord, thank You that You still give the same reward for tithing and giving abundantly that you gave thousands of years ago. You never change. I pray that you would bless my tithe to expand Your kingdom here on earth. In Jesus' name, Amen.

For Further Study

Mark 6:41–43, 2 Corinthians 9:7

08

CARING FOR GOD'S BRIDE

"For to everyone who has, more will be given, and he will have abundance; but from him who does not have, even what he has will be taken away." Matthew 25:29

Today, I want to give you an illustration that I hope will give you a fresh perspective on what tithing means to God and His kingdom.

Let's say I have to go on an extended journey, and I choose three men for a special responsibility. I say to those three men, "I'm going to send you each $10,000 every month. You may keep $9,000 of the money and spend it as you please. But I want you to give $1,000 each month to my wife to meet her needs."

As promised, I send each of these men $10,000 monthly. After a few months, I call my wife and ask her if she's receiving the support I arranged. She replies, "Well, the first one is sending $1,000 each month, just as you instructed him. The second one is actually sending $2,000 a month. I don't know why, but he is. But the third one sent $800 the first month, $300 the second month, and nothing the third month."

Now, as a husband who loves his wife with all his heart, what do you think I'm going to do? I am the one providing the money to these men. I've told them they can keep $9,000 for themselves. All I wanted them to do was give a mere 10 percent so that there could be food in my house.

Well, with the first man who was being faithful to follow my instructions, I am going to continue sending him $10,000. But for the third man—the one who wasn't satisfied with the 90 percent I graciously gave him—I am going to quit sending him $10,000 a month and send it to the most generous man instead. Why? *Because I can trust the second man.* He has demonstrated that he cares about what I care about. He is a good steward.

What the third man was doing was the same as stealing from me. Remember Malachi 3:8, which says, "Will a man rob God? Yet you have robbed Me! But you say, 'In what way have we robbed You?' In tithes and offerings."

Now let me bring this illustration home. Jesus has gone away for a season of time. He has said to each of us, "I want you to take care of My Bride (the Church) while I am away by giving 10 percent to My house. You can spend the remaining 90 percent as you desire."

Those who obey will be blessed. Those who go above and beyond will be blessed even more. But for those who refuse to do even the minimum, He's going to take what they have and give it to someone who will be a good steward with it.

The rewards of good stewardship are great, and God doesn't change. Tithing remains an extraordinary opportunity for blessing and abundance for those with the faith to trust Him. It is also the foundation upon which all the other principles I'm about to share with you are built. The blessed life awaits you. However, it begins with a heart commitment to honor, obey, and bless the Lord with your tithe.

....

Prayer

God, thank You for Your love for the Church. Help me to be a good steward of the money You've put in my possession. Thank You that through the tithe Your kingdom can advance and I can be blessed. In Jesus' name, Amen.

For Further Study

Luke 16:10–12; Matthew 25:21; Malachi 3:10

THE PRINCIPLE
OF MULTIPLICATION

"Then He took the five loaves and the two fish, and looking up to heaven, He blessed and broke them, and gave them to the disciples to set before the multitude."
Luke 9:16

Have you ever wished you could multiply your money? Well, I have wonderful news for you: God can do it. In fact, God is *the* Master of multiplication. One of my favorite examples of this comes from Luke 9:12–17, which tells the story of Jesus feeding the 5,000. You are probably very familiar with this story, but let's modernize and personalize it a bit. You may see some things you have never noticed before.

Picture yourself as one of the disciples. One day, an enormous crowd gathers. Counting the heads of households, you come up with about 5,000 men plus women and children. That means there are probably 15,000 to 20,000 people gathered on the hillsides listening to Jesus. He preaches all morning, and you expect Him to wrap up around noon, but He doesn't—He keeps right on teaching.

You think, *He's preaching well and everyone seems to be enjoying it. We'll let Him go a little bit longer today.* Then one o'clock, two o'clock, three o'clock, and four o'clock all come and go, and He continues expounding on the Scriptures! By five o'clock, you're beginning to hear from your associates: "The people are hungry, and all the restaurants are going to close soon!" The fact is, you're not sure whether it's really the people who are hungry or just your associates. But, being pretty famished yourself, you go to Jesus.

"Lord, please excuse the interruption, but the people haven't eaten all day, and now the restaurants are closing. So, we were thinking that You might want to . . . You know, uh . . . dismiss the service." He turns to you and says, "Give them something to eat," and then returns to His teaching. You go back to your associates and tell them what Jesus said.

So, you and the other disciples see how much food you can scrounge up, and 30 minutes later all you have is two fish sticks, five hushpuppies, and a Long John

Silver's kid's meal with a SpongeBob SquarePants action figure. It's not looking good. You return to Jesus to tell Him the disappointing news and He says, "That's great! Have the people sit down in groups of 50."

Have you ever watched 12 guys try to organize 20,000 men, women, and children into groups of 50? Herding cats across Texas would be a breeze by comparison. Once the people are in groups, Jesus takes the fish and hushpuppies, blesses them, breaks them in half, hands them back to you and the disciples and says, "Now go give it away." You look down at the broken piece of hushpuppy and wonder how it will stretch to feed all these people. But as you break off piece after piece, you realize a miracle is happening. This is one of the most remarkable things about this story—the miracle happened *in the disciples' hands*, not in Jesus' hands. You probably know how the story ends—everyone ate and there were 12 baskets of food left over.

Now, I've taken some creative liberties with this story because I want you to really see what happened. But I also hope to explain two key principles of multiplication in this story.

First, we see that something must be blessed before it can multiply. As we know from previous days, the way that our money is blessed and redeemed is by giving our firstfruits, or our tithe. Jesus, the One who receives our tithes, is the only One who has the power to bless it so that it can multiply.

The second principle of multiplication is this: Only what is given away can multiply. If the disciples had simply kept the food for themselves, it would've never multiplied. The same principle applies to our finances. When we give over and above our tithe, that's when our finances have the potential to multiply.

I hope this day's topic sheds some light on life-changing multiplication principles that could have a big impact on your finances and an even bigger impact on the kingdom of God.

....

Prayer
Lord, thank You for Your principle of multiplication and for letting me take part in the miracle You're doing in my finances. I pray that You will continue to multiply everything I give and increase my ability to be a giver. In Jesus' name, Amen.

For Further Study
Luke 9:12–17; Romans 11:16; Philippians 4:19

THE POWER OF OFFERINGS

"Will a man rob God? Yet you have robbed Me! But you say, 'In what way have we robbed You?' In tithes and offerings." Malachi 3:8.

Y esterday, I introduced the principles of multiplication by telling a modern-day, humorous version of the story of Jesus feeding the 5,000. Today, I want to continue talking about these principles by explaining the difference between tithing and giving.

Let's take a look at Matthew 25, in which Jesus tells a story of three stewards. One steward was entrusted with five talents. When accounting time came around, he returned those five talents to the Lord, plus five more. And in verse 21 the Lord said, "Well done, good and faithful servant." There was another steward who was entrusted with two talents, and, likewise, he returned to the Lord more than He had given him. But then there is the third steward—the one who was entrusted with one talent. In verse 25 he said to the Lord, "There you have what is yours." He only returned to the Lord what was already His. And the Lord called him a wicked and lazy servant.

Now, please don't misunderstand me. I'm not suggesting that anyone who *only* tithes is wicked and lazy. I am saying, however, there is a principle of faithful stewardship that teaches us we should give more to God than just the tithe, because tithing is simply returning to Him what is already His.

Of course, if you're not currently tithing, that is certainly the place to start. Tithing is where we remove the curse. It's what brings the blessing on the balance of our finances. Tithing is what causes God to rebuke the devourer and open the windows of heaven. It's the foundation on which our giving is built.

But if you look closely at today's verse, God is talking about more than just the tithe. He mentions "tithes and offerings." In other words, it's tithes *and* offerings that remove the curse. It's tithes *and* offerings that bring the blessings. It's tithes *and* offerings that rebuke the devourer. Because the firstfruits actually belong to the Lord, tithing isn't really giving—it's returning. To truly give, we have to go beyond our tithe. That's when we see the principle of multiplication in action.

I'm convinced God wants to bless and multiply our finances—just as He blessed and multiplied the two fish and the five loaves we talked about yesterday. The truth is that God can cause our finances to go further than we ever could through our own cleverness or diligence. I know this is true, because I've seen it operate in my own life over and over.

God wants your finances to be blessed, and He wants your finances to be multiplied. But it's vital to understand that you will never see the multiplication of your finances until you understand these two principles:

1. We give to the Lord first so that our finances are blessed.

2. We give over and above our tithes because only that which is shared can be multiplied.

These are the principles of multiplication. And they are as powerful today as they were on that Galilean hillside when Jesus fed the 5,000 with just two fish and five loaves of bread.

Prayer

God, thank You for blessing me and entrusting me with Your money. Give me faith to be a generous giver and to give over and above the tithe. Cause what I give to multiply and expand Your kingdom. In Jesus' name, Amen.

For Further Study

Matthew 25; Malachi 3:8–12; Luke 6:38

BREAKING THE SPIRIT OF MAMMON

"No one can serve two masters; for either he will hate the one and love the other, or else he will be loyal to the one and despise the other. You cannot serve God and mammon." Matthew 6:24

The word "mammon" is in the Bible four times, and three of those times Jesus said it. But what does it mean? Today, I want to talk to you about the spirit of mammon, because I think it's crucial to having a biblical view of money.

"Mammon" is an Aramaic word that essentially means "riches." At its heart there's an attitude that says: Man doesn't need God—we're self-sufficient. This is what the spirit of mammon tries to tell us: You don't need God. Trust in riches!

You may recognize "mammon" from the New Testament. In Matthew 6:24, Jesus clearly suggests it's *possible* to serve mammon instead of serving God, but He goes even further: Jesus states it is *impossible* to serve both at the same time. He says you will love one and hate the other. According to Jesus, there is no middle ground—no half-and-half.

Did you know all money has a spirit on it? It either has the Spirit of God or the spirit of mammon. Money that is submitted to God and His purposes has the Spirit of God on it. On the other hand, money that is not submitted to God has the spirit of mammon by default. That's why people think money can bring them happiness or fulfillment. Mammon is basically the spirit of the world—and that spirit is a liar.

I've noticed that the people most under the influence of the spirit of mammon tend to have the most fear about their money. As Jesus clearly suggests in today's verse, mammon tries to take the very place of God. Pastor Jimmy Evans, founder of MarriageToday and a Gateway apostolic elder, once said, "Mammon promises us those things that only God can give—security, significance, identity, independence, power, and freedom. Mammon tells us it can insulate us from life's problems and that money is the answer to every situation."

Clearly, this stands in direct opposition to the Spirit of God. For example, mammon says to buy and sell; God says to sow and reap. Mammon says to cheat and steal; God says to give and receive. Mammon tells you that if you had more money, people would listen to you, your relationship problems would go away, and life would be sweet. The differences between these two spirits seem very cut and dry; however, it's possible for believers to become influenced by the spirit of mammon without realizing it.

Mammon wants you to think, *If I just had more money, I could really start helping people and giving more to the kingdom.* Keep in mind, Jesus never told anyone the answer was more money. Money is not the answer to problems—God is. Now, don't get the wrong idea—money and mammon are not synonymous. Money is not inherently evil. One of the most frequently misquoted verses in the Bible is in 1 Timothy 6:10, which says, "For the love of money is a root of all kinds of evil."

Notice the Bible doesn't say *money* is the root of all kinds of evil. It says *the love of* money is a root of all kinds of evil. One of mammon's biggest tricks is getting us to trust in money rather than God. When you feel financial pressure, notice how the spirit of mammon tries to position itself as a substitute for God. It says, "You either need God to work a miracle right now or you need more money." That's simply a lie. We need God, period.

That's what Jesus is saying in Matthew 6:24. You can't serve two masters. You can't rely on both God and money to be your security and comfort. The Bible makes it clear that it's one or the other, and if I had to choose, I'd take God over any amount of money in the bank.

Prayer

God, I put my trust in You. Show me any area of my life in which You are not my source and help me to rely on You for my provision. There is no substitute for You in my life. I need You. In Jesus' name, Amen.

For Further Study

1 Timothy 6:6–10, 17; Hebrews 13:5; Psalm 62:10; Exodus 20:3

TRUE RICHES

"Do not lay up for yourselves treasures on earth, where moth and rust destroy and where thieves break in and steal; but lay up for yourselves treasures in heaven, where neither moth nor rust destroys and where thieves do not break in and steal. For where your treasure is, there your heart will be also." Matthew 6:19–21

Yesterday, we talked about how you can't serve two masters. In Luke 16:13, Jesus makes it clear that we can't serve both God and mammon at the same time. He says, "No servant can serve two masters; for either he will hate the one and love the other." But when we back up to verse 9, Jesus says something very important: "And I say to you, make friends for yourselves by unrighteous mammon, that when you fail, they may receive you into an everlasting home." In other words, we should use our earthly possessions to benefit others, so that when we die and leave our possessions behind, we'll be welcomed into heaven by those we helped.

We're instructed to use our money for that which is eternal. And what in our lives is eternal? People! The only lasting things we encounter each day are people. The human soul is eternal. That's why at Gateway our motto is "we're all about people." If I use my money to bring people to Christ, they'll welcome me into heaven when I die.

Notice in Luke 16:9, it doesn't say that *money* will welcome you. It says the friends you make will receive you into your everlasting home. I know one day I'm going to be greeted by people who are in heaven because I gave to churches, ministries, and missionaries that are bringing people to Christ. Just as He turned water into wine, God can turn money into souls. He's the only one who can turn unrighteous mammon into true riches.

In today's verse, Matthew 6:19–21, Jesus talks a lot about this, but He says it in a different way. He says, "Lay up for yourselves treasures in heaven." Luke 16:9 precisely instructs us how to put our treasure in heaven—by being good stewards on earth and using our money for righteous purposes. That's why I want to use it to invest in churches and ministries that are investing in people. I want my money to be used in helping people, loving people, feeding people, and caring for people.

But the enemy works hard to get us to store our treasures here on earth. He does this by corrupting and distorting our thoughts about money. He knows the more money we give to the church, the more souls are going to be saved, the more the kingdom of God will advance, and the kingdom of darkness is going to fail. And so he tries to get us to put our trust in money rather than in God so that we don't become more like our heavenly Father.

At this point, you might be thinking, *Well, I don't have any money so this giving stuff really doesn't apply to me.* I believe that having only a little bit of money gives us a great opportunity for blessing. In Luke 16:10, Jesus tells us, "He who is faithful in what is least is faithful also in much; and he who is unjust in what is least is unjust also in much." God is looking for people He can entrust with much, and He says that if you will be faithful with little, God will give you more. Later, in verse 12, Jesus says, "And if you have not been faithful in what is another man's, who will give you what is your own?"

What I'm trying to help us see is that it's not how much we have that matters—it's *whose* it is. All the money we have is His, not ours. Jesus tells me I need to be faithful with what is someone else's, because "if you have not been faithful in what is another man's, who will give you what is your own?" (Luke 16:12). When we obey Jesus' words in Luke 16, we are proving to God that we can be trusted with more, and even more importantly, we are truly putting our treasures in heaven.

Prayer
Lord, I want to use the money You've blessed me with to invest in eternal treasure, not temporary things. As I put my trust in You, help me direct my offerings—no matter how small or large—to Your righteous purposes. In Jesus' name, Amen.

For Further Study
1 Peter 4:10; Luke 12:42–48; Proverbs 11:28; Luke 16:9 (NLT)

MAMMON
HAS FRIENDS

"Blessed are those who don't feel guilty for doing something they have decided is right." Romans 14:22 (NLT)

Over the last few days, we've talked about the spirit of mammon and how it wants us to rely on riches rather than on God. The spirit of mammon has some friends, and today we're going to talk about the other spirits that often run in the same circles. Just as a spirit of mammon will keep you from living the blessed life, so will a spirit of poverty and a spirit of pride.

A spirit of poverty will cause you to be ashamed of the blessings of God. It makes you feel uncomfortable when receiving blessings from others or owning nice things. Because the devil can't stop God's blessings, he'll try to make you feel ashamed of them. I know this because I have experienced it myself. There was a time when God had to show me just how prevalent the poverty mentality was in my thinking. I remember purchasing a very nice golf jacket once that was just what I had wanted and needed. I found it at a golf shop at half price. I called Debbie from the pro shop to get her opinion, and she said, "It's a great deal. Buy it!"

I wore it directly out onto the golf course and proceeded to play some of the worst golf of my life. Of course, the spirit of poverty was quick to place the blame for my horrible score on the new jacket. *God didn't want you to have the nice jacket. You've missed God, and now your golf game is cursed!*

Believe it or not, as soon as the round was over, I returned the jacket and got my money back because I felt guilty wearing it. But that wasn't the end of it. In the days that followed, I began to grieve over "being forced" to return that jacket. I stewed about it, and I actually found myself resenting God. *I can't believe I can't even have a nice jacket. Other people get to have nice things, and I can't even buy a coat without my golf game being cursed. It's not fair God!* After putting up with this nonsense for about three days, God eventually got my attention and spoke very clearly, "Quit blaming Me for not having that jacket! I didn't tell you to take that jacket back." Then He said something I've never forgotten. The Lord said, "Son, I never speak to you through guilt or condemnation." (He also added, "And, by the way, don't blame Me for your lousy golf game.")

It's amazing to me that people feel the need to explain owning nice things. If you are a faithful, generous steward, you *will* be blessed. There is no avoiding it. As we have seen over and over in this devotional, the more you give away, the more God bestows. Think about this for a moment: Is there anything God could do in your life that you should feel ashamed of? Of course not!

Now, the other spirit that tends to hang around mammon is the spirit of pride. Pride says, "You've earned this stuff. Your hard work, ingenuity, and talent have made it happen. Thus, you should be *proud* of the blessings you have received." This sounds like the opposite of the spirit of poverty, but the two share a common root—they get us to focus on "stuff" rather than God. We become centered on the blessing rather than on the Blessor.

The spirit of pride says, "Wealth comes from hard work." The spirit of poverty says, "Wealth comes from the devil." The spirit of pride says, "You should be proud of what you have." The spirit of poverty says, "You should be ashamed of what you have." They are both traps because they are things-focused rather than God-focused. The key to staying God-focused with our finances is to put God first and have a heart of gratitude. This means tithing and being good stewards with what God has given you and not having to worry about explaining your blessings to others. Once the spirits of pride and poverty no longer have an influence in your life, you'll feel free to recognize and enjoy the blessings God has given you.

Prayer

Lord, thank You for blessing me. I realize that the spirit of poverty or pride may be affecting how I view Your blessings. In Your name, I rebuke those spirits and will no longer allow guilt, shame, or pride to ruin what You've intended for me to enjoy. In Jesus' name, Amen.

For Further Study

Psalm 62:10; Romans 8:1; Psalm 10:4

BASKETS
OF GRAIN

"Give, and it will be given to you: good measure, pressed down, shaken together, and running over will be put into your bosom. For with the same measure that you use, it will be measured back to you." Luke 6:38

Today's verse, Luke 6:38, is one of my favorite Scriptures. But I'm convinced it's one of the most frequently misapplied and misunderstood verses in the Bible. Many of the times I've heard preachers use this verse, it's during the offering time at church. However, one of the most common mistakes people make about this verse is thinking that Jesus is only speaking about money. In truth, He's revealing a principle that applies to every area of our lives.

To help us understand what Jesus means, let's back up and read verses 36 and 37: "You must be compassionate, just as your Father is compassionate. Do not judge others, and you will not be judged. Do not condemn others, or it will all come back against you. Forgive others, and you will be forgiven." Then, in verse 38, Jesus says, "Give, and it will be given to you." Yes, the verse does apply to money, but it also applies to forgiveness, mercy, understanding, and patience. Jesus is simply talking about the broad principle of giving. Whatever you give is going to be given back to you in "good measure, pressed down, shaken together, and running over."

The terms "good measure," "pressed down," "shaken together," and "running over" don't make a lot of sense the first time you hear them. But the people Jesus was talking to knew *exactly* what they meant.

According to instructions in the Old Testament, farmers in Israel were to leave the grain in the corners of their fields for the poor. So, each year at harvest time, there were two sets of harvesters in the field: the primary harvesters in the middle of the field who were paid to bring in the crop and the poor people in the corners who were harvesting the crop in order to feed themselves and their families.

Primary harvesters would fill up a basket, carry it over to the barn or wagon, then dump it out and go back to the field to begin filling the basket again. To these workers, it didn't really matter how full their baskets were, because they were being paid by the hour. They just needed to stay busy and keep working until all the grain was in the barn.

This wasn't the case for the poor people working in the corner of the field. They had probably walked several miles to get there. However much food they could get in their baskets would be the amount of food available to their families. If you were in that position, you would first make sure you had put in a good measure—or, in other words, filled the basket. Then you would press it down to create more room. After topping the basket off again, you would shake it to eliminate any air spaces between the grains. Having done all that, you would then pour in as much grain as you possibly could, heaping it up above the rim until it began to spill over the sides.

It is one thing to receive a basket of free grain. It is a far better thing to receive a good-measure, pressed-down, shaken-together, and running-over basket of free grain. Jesus used these terms because He wanted to communicate that whatever you give, you're going to get *a lot* more of the same in return.

Think about it this way. When you plant an apple seed, you don't just get back an apple seed. In time, you actually get back a whole apple tree, and on that tree are many apples, and each apple has many seeds. You get back so much more than you actually give! This is a universal principle with God. Keep it in mind as you look back over Luke 6:37. According to this principle, if you give judgment, much more will be given back to you. If you give condemnation, you'll get back much more. The good news is, if you give forgiveness and love, you'll receive much more of it than you actually gave.

The important thing to remember is that while God rewards our giving, it's not meant to be our motivation. God is looking at our hearts.

Prayer

Lord, thank You for Your generosity. Thank You that whatever we give—whether it's money, forgiveness, or mercy—You give back even more. Help me to be generous with more than just my finances. In Jesus' name, Amen.

For Further Study

Luke 6:38 (MSG); Deuteronomy 15:10; 1 Chronicles 29:14; Proverbs 11:25; 2 Corinthians 9:6

THE MOTIVE
OF GENEROSITY

"When you ask, you do not receive, because you ask with wrong motives, that you may spend what you get on your pleasures." James 4:3

Yesterday we talked about the meaning of Luke 6:38, which says, "Give, and it will be given to you: good measure, pressed down, shaken together, and running over." As I said, it's one of the most misunderstood passages in Scripture, and the biggest point of confusion has to do with our motivations.

I've heard so many people preach Luke 6:38 with material gain presented as the motive for giving. In reality, it shouldn't be our motivation—it should be the by-product. Let's take a look back at Luke 6:30, which says, "Give to everyone who asks of you. And from him who takes away your goods do not ask them back."

The message of Jesus' sermon in Luke 6:30–38 is *"Give!"* Give to those who ask of you. Give to those who can't pay you back. Give love to those who don't deserve it. Give mercy to those who wrong you. Give the kind of treatment you would hope to receive from others. Give, give, give! Oh, and by the way, when you do, your heavenly Father will make sure you get much more in return.

There is a subtle but important distinction in emphasis here. When you give with what looks to the world like reckless abandon, you are following God's example. God is a giver. We should give for the pure joy of imitating our wonderful Father. It's our hearts the Lord is concerned about. And a properly focused heart is more excited about the giving part than the receiving part. In other words, God is saying, "When you give just to give, I'm going to reward you by giving back to you in much greater measure." The reward comes because we have allowed God to do a work in our hearts in the area of *giving*—not in the area of *getting*.

There is an Old Testament glimpse of this truth in Deuteronomy 15:7-11, where God says:

> If there is among you a poor man of your brethren, within any of the gates in your land which the Lord your God is giving you, you shall not harden your heart nor shut your hand from your poor brother, but you

shall open your hand wide to him and willingly lend him sufficient for his need, whatever he needs. Beware lest there be a wicked thought in your heart, saying, "The seventh year, the year of release, is at hand," and your eye be evil against your poor brother and you give him nothing, and he cry out to the Lord against you, and it become sin among you. You shall surely give to him, and your heart should not be grieved when you give to him, because for this thing the Lord your God will bless you in all your works and in all to which you put your hand. For the poor will never cease from the land; therefore I command you, saying, "You shall open your hand wide to your brother, to your poor and your needy, in your land."

In this passage, we can clearly see God's heart for helping people. It also shows that God looks at the heart of the giver. He even makes it a point to tell the Israelites not to let their hearts "be grieved" when they give. God has always loved a cheerful giver.

It's not hard to understand why this is. Aren't you proud of your children when they're unselfish? Are you blessed when you have to bribe or threaten them to get them to be generous? We're pleased when our children help and prefer one another in love. And what is true for us as earthly parents is infinitely true for God.

When we grow to become cheerful, willing givers, we become more and more like our heavenly Father. But sometimes growth can require us to confront attitudes and motives that keep us from moving forward. God is trying to do a work in us. He wants to purify our hearts. And He does it by looking at our motives when we give.

Prayer
God, thank You that You give with reckless abandon. Make me more like You and give me Your heart for being generous and helping others. Help me to confront any attitudes that stand in the way of being a generous giver. In Jesus' name, Amen.

For Further Study
Proverbs 16:2; 1 Corinthians 4:5; Psalm 37:25–26; 2 Corinthians 9:10–12

THE RIGHT ATTITUDE

"Beware lest there be a wicked thought in your heart, saying, 'The seventh year, the year of release, is at hand,' and your eye be evil against your poor brother and you give him nothing, and he cry out to the Lord against you, and it become sin among you. You shall surely give to him, and your heart should not be grieved when you give to him, because for this thing the Lord your God will bless you in all your works and in all to which you put your hand." Deuteronomy 15:9–10

In today's passage, God clearly mentions two types of attitudes that we must confront to be cheerful givers like our heavenly Father: a selfish heart and a grieving heart.

Here God clearly labels selfish thoughts as wicked. Selfishness whispers that we won't have enough or that God won't be faithful to meet our needs if we give. God says, "Don't allow your heart to think that way." We are all selfish. The default condition of the human heart is to hoard and avoid sharing with anyone. For example, have you ever noticed that every English-speaking, two-year-old's favorite word is "mine"? We are completely and utterly self-absorbed from birth. Then a loving, heavenly Father comes to us and says, "I want to deal with this wicked, selfish heart and make you a giver. I want to make you like Me."

In Deuteronomy 15, after addressing the fact that we have a selfish heart, the second thing it says we have to deal with when it comes to giving is a grieving heart. God instructs us not to grieve after we've been obedient in giving. Selfishness can attack us *before* we give, but grief can attack us *after* we give.

Have you ever had buyer's remorse? Maybe you spent a lot of money on something such as a car or house, and after the excitement of the moment wore off, you experienced that panicky "what-have-I-done" feeling. As a result of this phenomenon, many of the items purchased on impulse are returned the following day.

Something similar can happen when you've been obedient to give as the Holy Spirit prompts. This often happens because people feel pressured to give rather than giving because it's their heart's desire. That means you have to guard your heart, not only before you give but afterward, as well.

So, how do you combat grief? You do it with a proper perspective regarding "your" money.

I once stopped right in the middle of a sermon and said, "I need someone to give me $100." Immediately, a man jumped up, came to the front, and handed me a one-hundred-dollar bill. I stuck the bill in my pocket and continued right on with my sermon. I'm sure every person in the congregation was thinking, *Why did he ask for $100? And why was that man so quick to get up and give it to him?* After letting everyone stew on it for several minutes, I explained. "Let me tell you why that gentleman was so quick to bring me $100 without knowing why I needed it. Before the service, I gave him a hundred-dollar bill and told him I would ask for it during the service and to bring it up quickly whenever I asked for it." The reason he gave the money promptly when I asked for it was because it was mine in the first place. He didn't experience grief, remorse, or emotional conflict about giving me the money. Why? *Because he knew it wasn't his.*

This illustration shows us exactly how we should steward the money God has given us. The truth is everything we have is God's, and when we know that in our hearts, we won't feel any grief when we give. Instead, we will feel joy and gratitude knowing God has blessed us so much that we can bless others.

....

Prayer

Lord, thank You for reminding me that everything I have is Yours. Help me to handle my money as a steward, not an owner, so that selfishness and grief do not keep me from being a cheerful giver. In Jesus' name, Amen.

For Further Study

Psalm 119:36; Psalm 50:9–10; 1 Timothy 6:10

A GENEROUS HEART

"You shall supply him liberally from your flock, from your threshing floor, and from your winepress. From what the Lord has blessed you with, you shall give to him."
Deuteronomy 15:14

One of my favorite sayings is, "I was born selfish, but I was born again generous." I can't begin to tell you how much joy giving has brought to our lives as a family. Being givers in God's kingdom is the most fun we have ever had. It has resulted in a more exciting life than we could ever have imagined.

Some time ago, Debbie was talking with a pastor and his wife who were staying in our home. They could clearly see that we were blessed, so the pastor asked my wife, "Why do you think God has blessed you so much?" Debbie thought about it a moment and answered, "I think it has to do with Robert's heart. When Robert got saved, God so changed his heart that he would give away everything we owned if he sensed God telling Him to do it. As a matter of fact, he's done it several times because he loves God and he loves people. The Lord has given him a heart that wants to give generously to God's people and God's work."

Now, I tell this story from a place of humility. To no credit of my own, this is a work God has done in me. He has changed my heart from being selfish to being liberal and generous. I'm not using the term "liberal" in the political sense. I'm talking about liberality—the practice of being generous and free with our material possessions. Take a look again at today's Scripture, which says, "You shall supply him liberally from your flock, from your threshing floor, and from your winepress."

We may not have threshing floors or winepresses nowadays, but we are still called to give liberally from what God has blessed us with. We are not to be stingy in our giving; we are to be generous. That's why we must cultivate a liberal heart. This goes against the grain of our fallen natures, but it's perfectly consistent with the new natures we received when we gave our lives to Jesus.

The key to walking in the new nature, rather than the old one, is simply a matter of renewing your mind. Romans 12:2 says, "And do not be conformed to this world, but be transformed by the renewing of your mind." Mind renewal brings transformation. Once we've been transformed in this area, there's one more work God must do in our hearts—we must develop a grateful heart.

Let's look at Deuteronomy 15:15: "You shall remember that you were a slave in the land of Egypt, and the Lord your God redeemed you; therefore I command you this thing today." Why did God instruct the Israelites to remember they had been slaves? Because it would fill their hearts with gratitude for what He had done for them. From time to time, in worship or in my quiet time, God reminds me of my past. He doesn't do it to produce guilt or condemnation. He does it to produce deep gratitude.

Many years ago, I was at a very small church speaking about giving. There was a young man there who had just recently come to know Christ. Prior to being born again, he had squandered all of his money and was essentially broke. At offering time, he said, *Lord, what can I give? I have so little money, but my heart is so full of gratitude for what You have done for me.* As he asked, the Lord gave him the idea of taking out a life insurance policy and making the church the beneficiary. So he arranged for a $100,000 policy. Just a few years later, he passed away, and the church received that money—a larger gift than he could possibly have given any other way. From his heart of gratitude came a huge blessing to that little church.

Just imagine what the Lord can do through us when we renew our minds to become generous, grateful givers! Today, I challenge you to ask Him to give you a grateful heart and see what opportunities He gives you to be generous.

Prayer
God, thank You for saving me and reminding me of how You rescued me. Give me a grateful heart and provide me with opportunities to be generous. In Jesus' name, Amen.

For Further Study
Deuteronomy 5:29; Proverbs 16:2

NEED, GREED, OR SEED

"But this I say: He who sows sparingly will also reap sparingly, and he who sows bountifully will also reap bountifully. So let each one give as he purposes in his heart, not grudgingly or of necessity; for God loves a cheerful giver. And God is able to make all grace abound toward you, that you, always having all sufficiency in all things, may have an abundance for every good work."
2 Corinthians 9:6–8

There was a remarkable 18-month period during which Debbie and I were able to give away nine vehicles. Every time we would give one away, God would provide another. During that time, I learned a valuable lesson about being a cheerful giver.

Someone who knew we had given away a number of vehicles approached us saying, "We have a spare vehicle, and we'd like to anonymously give it to a certain family." We agreed to take the vehicle and give it to the family, so they transferred the title to our ministry. As I was delivering the car to the recipients' house, the car's engine went out. I had to have the car towed to a garage and pay to have a new engine put in it. I recall doing a little complaining and grumbling to the Lord about that. I was saying, "Lord, why couldn't the engine have gone out just a few days earlier when those people still had the car—or a few days later after it was delivered to the people who were going to drive it? Why did it go out when it was in my possession?"

I remember the Lord speaking very clearly to me. "I planned it that way, son. The person who was giving the car away didn't have the money to put a new engine in it, and the family who was receiving the vehicle certainly didn't have the money to do it, but I have blessed you financially. You should be grateful that I've blessed you with the privilege of putting a new engine in the vehicle for that family." And then the Lord gave me a gentle warning, saying, "Now, if you're tired of being a blessing to other people, I can certainly direct those resources to someone else." Obviously,

I repented to the Lord and quickly went from being a "grudging, under compulsion" giver to being a cheerful one.

Paul talks about being a cheerful giver in today's Scripture, 2 Corinthians 9:6–8, which happens to be one of the Bible's most popular and important passages on giving. Keep in mind these words were directed to a group of people who were about to make a sacrificial offering. They were givers. Paul, writing under the direction of the Holy Spirit, begins by stating the most basic law of giving: "He who sows sparingly will also reap sparingly, and he who sows bountifully will also reap bountifully." In verse 7, Paul's very next phrase is an important one because he's giving us the primary guideline for giving. Each person is to give "as he purposes in his heart." You are the only person on earth who can decide what the right level of giving is for you. It's between you and God.

As Paul continues in verse 7, he says something very important about our attitudes as we give. Let's look at it in the New International Version: "Each man should give what he has decided in his heart to give, not reluctantly or under compulsion, for God loves a cheerful giver."

Paul makes it clear that God is not looking for tithes, offerings, and gifts that are given "reluctantly or under compulsion." The blessed life is an outgrowth of "cheerful" giving.

So, how do you become a cheerful giver? There is only one way: God must do a work in your heart. As with every other truth we've explored up to this point, it all comes down to the heart. We must allow God to replace our selfish and grieving hearts with generosity. When we do, Paul says "God is able to make all grace abound toward you, that you, always having all sufficiency in all things, may have an abundance for every good work" (2 Corinthians 9:8). To me, that truly sounds like the blessed life.

Prayer

Lord, thank You for Your promise to people who give cheerfully. Speak to me about how I should be generous, and do a work in my heart so I can obey You without reluctance or compulsion. Thank You for using my finances to do good works! In Jesus' name, Amen.

For Further Study

Deuteronomy 28:2; Psalm 37:26

THREE SEED PRINCIPLES

"The kingdom of God is as if a man should scatter seed on the ground, and should sleep by night and rise by day, and the seed should sprout and grow, he himself does not know how. For the earth yields crops by itself: first the blade, then the head, after that the full grain in the head. But when the grain ripens, immediately he puts in the sickle, because the harvest has come." Mark 4:26–29

There are three fundamental principles relating to seed that I want to tell you about.

1. You reap *what* you sow.

I'm sure you've heard this phrase before. It's a common saying because it's a self-evident truth. For example, if you sow corn, you reap corn; if you sow wheat, you reap wheat; and if, as Paul suggests, you sow money, you reap money. It's a law that was established at the creation of the world, which we read in Genesis 1:11–12:

> Then God said, "Let the earth bring forth grass, the herb that yields seed, and the fruit tree that yields fruit according to its kind, whose seed is in itself, on the earth"; and it was so. And the earth brought forth grass, the herb that yields seed according to its kind, and the tree that yields fruit, whose seed is in itself according to its kind. And God saw that it was good.

However, as glaringly obvious as this principle sounds, you'd be surprised how many times I've observed people expecting things to work some other way in their case. Can you imagine a farmer standing in a field in which he has sown wheat seeds and being frustrated because corn is not appearing? That would be foolishness. But that is precisely what so many believers do. They expect a harvest of something they've never planted. Let me emphasize once again, this is not a holy get-rich-quick scheme. We don't sow for the purpose of getting more money; however, financial growth is a by-product of bountiful sowing.

2. You reap *after* you sow.

This is the second principle you need to know. Once again, I know that seems mind-numbingly simple but you cannot believe how many people say things like, "Someday, when I have more money, I'm going be a giver." It will never happen. You can't reap *before* you sow. Once again, this is a principle God has woven into the natural order of things. Jesus affirms this in today's Scripture when He says, "The kingdom of God is as if a man should scatter seed on the ground, and should sleep by night and rise by day, and the seed should sprout and grow."

Imagine the same foolish farmer I mentioned earlier now standing in the field waiting for a crop to come in when he has never planted a seed. "Once this crop comes up, I'm going to do some serious sowing," he says confidently. "I'll be a big-time sower if I ever get this crop to come in." Of course, this is absurd. Yet I have heard many believers say pretty much the same thing, such as, "If God will help me close this major business deal, I'm really going to start giving to the church." It's the one who is faithful with little who will receive much. You have to start where you are.

3. You reap *more* than you sow.

The essence of this principle can be found in Psalm 126:5-6, which says, "Those who sow in tears shall reap in joy. He who continually goes forth weeping, bearing seed for sowing, shall doubtless come again with rejoicing, bringing his sheaves with him." As this passage implies, the principle of harvest increase is so powerful that, even if you're crying as you scatter your little bag of precious seed, your tears will turn to rejoicing as you begin bringing in your sheaves of harvest.

Think about it—just a few kernels of planted corn will produce a stalk with several ears. And each ear will contain hundreds of seed kernels (approximately 400 kernels). That's a pretty good return, isn't it?

You always get more when you sow God's way, but it's up to us to take the first step. That starts with being faithful in planting the first seed. It may be difficult to take the first step, but once you do you'll be rewarded with much more than you ever expected.

Prayer

Lord, thank You for creating these seed principles. In Your kingdom, one small seed produces more than I can imagine, so help me to bountifully sow good seed. In Jesus' name, Amen.

For Further Study

Job 4:8; Proverbs 11:18; Galatians 6:8

THE LADDER
OF GIVING

"You can pray for anything, and if you have faith, you will receive it." Matthew 21:22 (NLT)

A few years ago, I made a breakthrough discovery. I saw something in the Word about giving that I had never seen before. I saw that for the Christian, there are actually three levels of giving to the Lord:

1. Tithes
2. Offerings
3. Extravagant Offerings

Soon after discovering this hierarchy of giving, I excitedly called a friend of mine—a person with a strong gift of giving—to share it with him. I said, "The Lord has shown me something I've never seen before. Did you know that there are three levels of giving?" Very matter-of-factly, he said, "Yes, I did, and I can even tell you what they are." I remember thinking, *Wrong, Mr. Smarty Pants. I just got this fresh from heaven. I've never heard it preached or taught at any time. There is no way you know what I'm about to say.*

So I called his bluff. "All right, then, what are they?" He said, "Tithes, offerings, and painful offerings." He had phrased it a little less delicately than I had, but that was it! He knew! Sadly, most believers don't know about these three levels of giving because, as I've already mentioned, they rarely even get to the first level. Consequently, they never even get a glimpse of the joy, fun, and blessing available at the higher levels. However, over the years, I have observed that those who do get to the first level usually move on to the next one. Why? Because tithing removes the curse and opens the windows of heaven over us. So, when we start tithing, we're much more likely to start giving offerings as the Lord leads us.

Nevertheless, very few Christians will ever reach the third level of giving to the Lord—the level of extravagant giving—and this is a tragedy. Some of the most remarkable people in the Bible were extravagant givers. Take King David, who gave an extravagant offering to the Lord so his son Solomon could build the Temple.

Converted to today's currency, his offering would amount to $21 billion. If that's not extravagant, I don't know what is.

In 1 Kings 3, there's another example of an extravagant gift. Solomon became known around the world for being extremely wise. Do you remember how Solomon received that wisdom? He had just been set in as king, and the tradition was to sacrifice a bull, but do you know what Solomon did instead? He sacrificed 1,000 bulls! Because of this, God came to him and said, "Ask anything of Me, and I'll give it to you." He did this because Solomon demonstrated that he had a generous, unselfish heart. He was a giver.

I can assure you that a person who is not a giver at the highest level is not likely to have God come to him and say, "Ask anything." He can't, because He hasn't had the opportunity to do a work in his heart. He could not trust him with the blank check He handed to Solomon.

Here's another extravagant gift in the Bible. This one rivals that of David and Solomon combined. We find it in Luke 21:2, which says, "And He [Jesus] saw also a certain poor widow putting in two mites." That's right. A poor widow with her offering of two mites made the extravagant gift list because, according to Jesus, it was all she had. It took as much, or more, faith for her to give two mites as it did for David to give $21 billion in gold! It's not the amount; it's the heart. Two pennies constitute an extravagant gift when they are all you have.

In Genesis 22, we read about another extravagant gift on a remote hilltop in what would one day become Jerusalem, a man named Abraham prepared to offer up his only, miraculous son. I'd call that extravagant. I'll give you one even better than that: Not too far away from that hilltop, 2,000 years later, God Himself offered His only, blameless Son as a sacrifice for our freedom and lives. I'd call that an extravagant gift. I'll use my friend's word and call that a painful gift.

God has made it abundantly clear all through the Bible that He is the ultimate extravagant giver. He is generous, and He wants to do a work in our hearts that makes us more like Him.

....

Prayer

God, thank You for extravagantly giving us Your greatest gift: Jesus. Give me the faith and the heart to give just like David, Solomon, and the widow who gave all she had. Remove any attitude that keeps me from being an extravagant giver. In Jesus' name, Amen.

For Further Study

Genesis 22:1–19; 1 Kings 3:4–13

A PURPOSE
FOR EVERY GIFT

"Then Mary took a pound of very costly oil of spikenard, anointed the feet of Jesus, and wiped His feet with her hair. And the house was filled with the fragrance of the oil." John 12:3

Thirty years ago, I had some friends who were newly married, deeply in love, and flat broke. They had no money, no savings, *nothing*. One day, my friend received a surprise bonus check from his job. It was the largest amount of money they had ever seen in one lump sum. To them it was a huge amount, especially since they didn't really have anything. They had lots of needs and plenty of ways to spend the money, but once the euphoria subsided, they started sensing the money wasn't for them.

They went to the pastor of the church and said, "We don't know specifically who or what this is for, but we want to give this money." Then their pastor said, "Yesterday, I met with a widow in our church. I found out they are going to take her house if she can't come up with a certain amount of money. The amount she needs, to the penny, is the amount of this check."

The reason I'm telling you this story is to show that God has a purpose for every gift. This is a biblical truth we see in John 12:1–8, in which Mary gave Jesus an extravagant gift.

> Then, six days before the Passover, Jesus came to Bethany, where Lazarus was who had been dead, whom He had raised from the dead. There they made Him a supper; and Martha served, but Lazarus was one of those who sat at the table with Him. Then Mary took a pound of very costly oil of spikenard, anointed the feet of Jesus, and wiped His feet with her hair. And the house was filled with the fragrance of the oil. But one of His disciples, Judas Iscariot, Simon's son, who would betray Him, said, "Why was this fragrant oil not sold for three hundred denarii and given to the poor?" This he said, not that he cared for the poor, but because he was a thief, and had the money box; and

he used to take what was put in it. But Jesus said, "Let her alone; she has kept this for the day of My burial. For the poor you have with you always, but Me you do not have always."

Think about the extravagance of the gift Mary gave Jesus. Three hundred denarii was equal to about a year's wages. Imagine taking all the money you make in a year and spending it on perfumed oil. Now, imagine taking that oil and pouring it on someone's feet. You're never going to get it back. It begs the question, *Why?*

When we go back to the chapter before this story, John 11, we see a detailed account of Jesus coming to Bethany and raising Mary and Martha's brother Lazarus from the dead. One chapter later, Mary gave her most precious possession to the Lord. Is it possible that the events of chapter 11 gave Mary a new perspective? Could burying her beloved brother, having him lie in the grave for four days, and then suddenly seeing him restored to life at the word of Jesus have changed Mary's values and priorities? Maybe material possessions didn't seem so precious anymore. Perhaps our perspective needs to change as well. After all, if you know Jesus, you've been raised from the dead yourself (Ephesians 2:4–6). See, a generous heart stems from a grateful heart.

In Mark's account of this story, in Mark 14:8, he records some of Jesus' words that John didn't. This is where we realize that Mary's gift had a deeper purpose than she could have imagined. After Judas complained about the "waste" of the precious oil, Jesus responded by saying, "She has done what she could. She has come beforehand to anoint My body for burial."

If you recall the details of the crucifixion, you'll remember that Jesus' body was taken off the cross at sundown just before the Sabbath was about to begin. That meant they had to quickly wrap Jesus' body in cloth and lay Him in the tomb. There was no time to anoint His body with perfumed oils or spices as they normally would. Think about it: The only person on earth who received the privilege of anointing Jesus' body for burial was Mary.

You never know the purpose behind your gift. But if God puts it in your heart to give extravagantly, and you obey, you'll be amazed by the way He uses your gift.

Prayer
God, thank You that the gifts I give have a purpose. Give me a grateful and generous heart, and cause my gifts to be used for Your kingdom in miraculous, powerful ways. In Jesus' name, Amen.

For Further Study
Ephesians 2:4–6; John 11:1-44

ROBERT MORRIS is the founding senior pastor of Gateway Church, a multicampus, evangelistic, Spirit-empowered church in the Dallas/Fort Worth Metroplex. Since it began in 2000, the church has grown to more than 36,000 active members. He is featured on the weekly television program, *The Blessed Life*, broadcast to approximately 100 million homes in the United States and more than 200 countries around the world. Robert holds a doctorate of literature and serves as chairman of the board of The King's University. He is the bestselling author of 11 books, including *The Blessed Life*, *From Dream to Destiny*, *The God I Never Knew*, and *The Blessed Church*. Robert and his wife, Debbie, have been married 34 years and are blessed with one married daughter, two married sons, and five grandchildren. You can follow Robert on Twitter @PsRobertMorris.